D0719596

The DERANGED Book

for Old-Timers

Marcus Waring

MARKS &
SPENCER

Marks and Spencer plc
PO Box 3339
Chester CH99 9QS

s h o p   o n l i n e

www.marksandspencer.com

ISBN: 978-1-84024-691-9
Printed in Great Britain

The views in this book are those of the author but they are general views only and readers are urged to consult a relevant and qualified specialist for individual advice in particular situations. Marks and Spencer p.l.c. hereby exclude all liability to the extent permitted by law for any errors or omisissions in this book and for any loss, damage or expense (whether direct or indirect) suffered by a third party relying on any information contained in this book.

First published in 2008 by Summersdale Publishers Ltd

The right of Marcus Waring to be identified as the author of this work has been asserted in accordance with sections 77 and 78 of the Copyright, Designs and Patents Act 1988.

Condition of Sale

Contents

Introduction

There goes Father Time again. With his dodgy back and long-handled scythe, which has Health and Safety reaching for their clipboards, this wizened figure has long been associated with the cycle of life. While you work, rest and buy inexpensive undergarments he lurks backstage, moving the years quietly along and trying to get the number of the pretty girl in the costume department. Until the day comes when you hit 60, look in the mirror and realise you are officially an old-timer.

Beyond general panic, birthday cakes dangerously overloaded with candles and lying through your (possibly false) teeth about your true vintage, there is something rather neat about time. Whether you are rich or poor, happy or selling double glazing over the telephone, it is the ultimate system that can't be cheated, the one rule that can't be fooled with. You may tinker with the engine, but one day the head gasket is going to blow. In the future, scientists might crack the codes of old age and 1,000-year-old citizens will stride the earth, quietly stealing all the decent moisturiser and thrashing everyone at pub quizzes. But for now, there is an unshakeable direction to our lives that we must deal with. From the queen of England to the person who sold you this book, one day we will all be somewhere else – hopefully Maui.

In your thirties and forties, you might have thought the clock was racing, but now it seems to be using banned substances as well, and getting on in life brings change. Perhaps you've noticed that young people no longer give you a second glance in the street, but this is to their folly. Many of the more senior citizens among us have been everywhere, done most of it, and emerged a bit wobbly but otherwise intact. They might have holes in their cardigans but by God do they know how to re-pot cyclamens.

It might have been fun and games to make catapults or learn about fossils when you were young and hearty, but what about now you are starting to feel a bit fossilised yourself? You just know you are going to suffer a ghastly accident if you attempt to make a tree house. *The Deranged Book for Old-timers* seeks to find those other, more sedate pleasures, from exploring the afternoon snooze to how to twitch curtains properly. It is time to blow a raspberry at Death and give Father Time a firm kick up the bum. Yes, we are going to grow old, but we are going to make sure we do it disgracefully.

Chapter One

Essential Clutter

When you were young, you wouldn't have dreamt of disappearing into the woods for a day of derring-do without childhood essentials such as a penknife, three marbles and a rhubarb and custard chew (with bits of fluff stuck to it). The canny old-timer also knows there are certain things that are essential to help you get through the day, some of them in the home and others for when you venture outside.

Things to have on you

Reading glasses

The origin of glasses is as hazy as the stuff people try to see without them. They are said to be the brainchild of a thirteenth-century Florentine monk, although there is also evidence from the first century AD that Roman Emperor Nero looked through an emerald to help him watch gladiators doing each other a bit of harm. Whether these stories are true or not, the fact remains that as we age our eyesight grows weaker, along with our ability to understand remote controls. This means having a pair of glasses to hand becomes vital if you want to see what you are reading. There are some pitfalls, however:

1. Installing a pair in every room is a good idea, but be prepared for small, mischievous ghosts who will permanently hide your glasses in obscure places, sometimes within seconds of you putting them down.

2. Keeping them on your head doesn't always work – you soon forget they are there and find yourself wandering the house for hours, looking in drawers and dusty compartments, and getting increasingly agitated.

3. Having an extra pair can be a double-edged sword. In senior moments, the aged have even been known to put a second pair on their nose when the first is already resting there. This could be due to nose numbness, which is a result of excessive blowing (see Tissues, below), but we can't be certain.

4. Getting chains so you can hang the glasses round your neck is a fine idea, but with two drawbacks. One is you catch half your lunch in them – although this can be a nice surprise when you are doing the crossword and become peckish at around 4 p.m. Bear in mind that getting caught sucking your

glasses chain is not sexy. The other is you can easily catch the chain on door and cupboard handles, neatly garrotting yourself in the process, but saving the NHS and your family a lot of hassle and cash.

> **Try this:** if you suddenly find yourself stranded in the Australian outback or the wilds of Canada, attach a hook to your glasses chain and use it to catch small, gullible fish.

Tissues

Tissues are hugely important. Where once it would have been a monogrammed cotton handkerchief, nowadays it is paper tissues from the likes of Kleenex that have cleaned up in this lucrative market. Like miniature fluffy friends, steady streams of these have stuffed the sleeves of the elderly for years. Your grandchildren will be amazed at the seemingly inexhaustible supply, and they will go wide-eyed with a mixture of surprise and horror when a used one falls out onto the table during Sunday lunch. Remember to always keep your sleeves adequately loaded. The grandchildren might hold you responsible for the demise of trees that have got the chop just to soak up your sexagenarian snuffles, but you can counter-attack with the news that the young sniffle and blow as much as you. Note that since the sexual revolution, ladies can use man-sized tissues without fear of a reprisal.

> **Try this:** if you want to cut a dash, go retro and get real cotton handkerchiefs with your initials on them. These can be useful at funerals, especially if you are looking for a prospective partner, since they mark you out as an individual of distinction and you can make your move while the other person is teary and vulnerable.

Pills

The youth of today might carry pills as well, but these are to be avoided as there's a good chance taking Ecstasy will make you lose your already scattered marbles. But having a bottle of medicinal ones on your person can be doubly useful sometimes; not only will they calm your boiling blood pressure when you glimpse the rippling torso of a builder in the high street or the smooth legs of that lovely girl in the hairdresser's, they are also useful for shaking at fractious grandchildren when they become a pain in the bum.

> **Try this:** a bottle of pills can make a wonderful rattle for scaring cats out of your shrubbery.

Diary

As the years race by, keeping a diary becomes essential to record all those exciting events you struggle to remember. Forget the electronic gadgetry of palmtops (something to do with trees?), and BlackBerry mobile devices (not as good for you as their namesake). What you need is a slim, dependable paper diary to scribble in with your increasingly erratic handwriting. Writing badly becomes useful when arguments arise over an important date or event, because sometimes your handwriting is so unreadable that you can force a truce. The battleground where the diary swings into action is a time-honoured setting – you are sitting there with your husband or wife and the conversation turns to when John and Peggie visited last August: 'No dear, it was September.' The opening shot is fired, troops are mobilised. And so to the diary, that oracle of truth, where it turns out it *was* August. The sad thing is this matters in later years because not enough serious stuff is going on, and arguing over trivia becomes something of a delicious obsession, rather like scratching an insect bite.

> **Try this:** if you are losing an argument over when you last washed the car, switch tactics and use the diary to slap the offending person on the head.

All change please

Make sure you have some cash on you for unexpected visits from your children as they will bring young, greedy grandchildren who view you as a kind of slow-moving bank. The regular dispensing of high-denomination coins will soon give way to notes. These kids have mobile phones to run, for goodness' sake.

Try this: forget the offspring and blow the lot on Horlicks and lottery scratchcards.

Things to have near you

Walking stick

Walking sticks have a lengthy and distinguished history. Originally employed by shepherds to clout thieves or sheep, walking sticks gained social prestige, meaning you were regarded as someone of clout yourself if you posessed one. Fancy versions, like a full-blown ceremonial mace, while somewhat ostentatious, will certainly have curtains twitching and the neighbours wondering if you won at bingo last Saturday. Add a crown to the ensemble and you've got yourself a powerful P. Diddy bad-ass rapper image, which will cause Mrs Beatty at number 45 to have another one of her funny turns – funny for everyone else, anyway.

The uses of the stick are varied. If you are ex-military, whacking the side of your leg with it (preferably the one with the metal plate) while barking at your peers in the street is considered good form in upper social circles. The stick can lend you an air of authority when pointing to things, especially when being asked directions by strangers. It also gently reminds them that you are armed and possibly confused, and should not be trifled with. This also applies when you are visited by door-to-door salesmen flogging 'made in China' shower caps and Jehovah's Witnesses – although why anyone would want to buy a Jehovah's Witness remains unclear.

In the same family as sticks and often made of bamboo or rattan, canes came about in the seventeenth century as a slightly less aggressive replacement for a large, sharp sword. A swift bop on the head was at least better than losing one's head entirely. Canes are similarly dignified, hinting at wartime injuries and devilish exploits as a youth which have now trashed your joints and rendered you unsteady on your pins. Arguably their finest use came into being when some ingenious fellow hollowed out a compartment near the top and installed a sneaky little flask of alcohol. This type of cane became known as a tippler. It has saved many old-timers from having to do the washing-up on Christmas Day by helping them to get mysteriously more pissed and unreliable with the crockery than everyone else put together.

Try this: the crook of a walking stick is very useful for picking up things like dogs or small children.

The long-handled shoehorn

Another stroke of genius is the shoehorn, which first appeared in the fifteenth century. Elizabethans would have been particularly happy with one of these gizmos as they had silly, tight-fitting shoes, which sometimes made them ill-tempered and their faces blotchy. Early shoehorns were made primarily from animal bone or horn, which gave them their uncomplicated name. Then someone really started showing off and came up with the long-handled shoehorn. With one of these you can slip on your shoes without bending down, creaking and moaning and making yourself feel ten years older. Ideally, the shoehorn should hang near the shoes and the back door.

Try this: they also double up as paddles for kinky spanking when there is nothing worth watching on the television.

TV guide

Someone once said that life was too long to go without TV, and they may have a point. Reading is essential, radio a lifeline and doing the crossword good for preventing your brain from caving in altogether, but sometimes it's nice to have some life in the room that isn't asleep in a chair. Cue the idiot box. Whether you're ranting at the feckless desperadoes on *Big Brother* and wondering at the state of British society today or enjoying the timeless delights of *Dad's Army* and the ever-panicking Captain Mainwaring, the TV guide puts you back in the driving seat – or comfortable armchair with matching footstool.

> **Try this:** roll up the TV guide and use it as a rudimentary bat to play peanut cricket with your loved one. If they catch one in their mouth, you are out.

The Oldie

Like the TV guide, having a copy of *The Oldie* means you know the score. It will keep you up to speed with what's going on in the world of the aged with waspy reviews of plays, discourse on why you don't want to visit Mustique and happy snaps of society's high-rollers. Sure, one day you will be ashes scattered in the wind, but you want to dance on that wind as well-informed dust rather than fall out of the sky like unintelligent soot.

> **Try this:** make the pages into paper aeroplanes of increasing complexity, incorporating wing flaps and Sidewinder missiles. Then bombard your neighbours with them.

Rug

In your eighties and nineties a rug becomes your best friend, especially when winter winds blast down from the Arctic, bringing snow and chilblains. At this dark time of year, just looking out of the window makes you start thinking un-Christian thoughts about your neighbours basking by their pool in Alicante. If you are wealthy, lucky or have robbed a bank, you might sun yourself in southern Spain or be a 'snowbird' wintering over in Florida where rugs are not acceptable accessories unless you are close to snuffing it. In northern Europe it is important to wrap a length of tartan around your knees to keep yourself warm, while looking smugly and snugly at the rain and wind lashing the bare trees outside. Lambswool and mohair are sound options, or you can pick up a tartan knee rug from under £20 online. But a word of caution for the 'rewired retired' who are getting the hang of this Internet thingy: you will have also bought yourself a one-handed electric food grater for £35.95 quicker than you can say 'pointless crap'.

Try this: if your blanket is red, use it to goad bulls in a field at the nearest farm. The police will give you a severe telling off – that's if you make it out alive.

Chapter Two

The Grey Matters

Once you have partially or totally retired, you have a lot of time on your hands – sometimes too much. Tales abound of former captains of industry descending to the factory floor of despair when they realise they can't spend all day fiddling with the chrysanthemums and avoiding watching *Bargain Hunt*. The irony is dreadful – you spend your working life looking forward to retirement, only to lose the plot and fall to bits when you get there. So find yourself a few stimulating hobbies to keep your mind busy.

Doing the crossword

A Liverpudlian journalist, Arthur Wynne, invented the modern crossword, jauntily known as a 'word-cross', in 1913 for *New York World*. But this addictive form of word puzzle is thought to go back much further. A version of a crossword has been found inscribed on an ancient tomb in

Egypt. One down's clue was 'A collection of locusts, sounds a bit like vague', and the answer was 'plague' – they had weeks of laughter with that. Then someone got carried away with 'A female ruler with really bad teeth', Queen Hatshepsut got to hear of this and everything went horribly wrong for someone.

Wynne's idea fired the public imagination, and the *Sunday Express* was the first British newspaper to include one in 1924. Nowadays most newspapers carry them, and newsagents have a clutch of brightly coloured puzzle books to keep you going. One is never enough. *The Independent* and *The Daily Telegraph* quick crosswords always use the first two words across to make a phrase or name, which is a delightful trick to teach your grandchildren, who won't know about it. They will have a new-found respect for you and it is good for their word power. So when they next send a text message to their friends by mobile phone, they can use the word 'arbitrary' and get the baffled reply 'u wot m8?', before being beaten silly when they are next in the school playground – now look what you have done.

With a stout thesaurus and lots of time to spare, the quick crossword is just a gentle warm-up for the cryptic one, where clues like 'Mushroom that is bathed in electric moonlight, say' will actually mean something. The beauty of it is once you have got into this mindset, this sort of thing is a breeze and many young whippersnappers do not have a clue how to do it.

Difficult words:

Azimuth – an angular distance measured along a horizon of an object from north or south points. We knew that.

Fanfaronade – boasting, or a blast of trumpets. This is common in gentlemen's toilets.

Megachiroptera – to do with a fruit bat, known as *Megachiropterous*. Of course.

Wayzgoose – the company 'do', such as a dinner, typically used among printing firms. Why call it the office piss-up when you can get geese involved?

Llanfairpwllgwyngyllgogerychwyrndrobwllllantysiliogogogoch
– the 58-letter Welsh town is the longest word ever used in a published crossword. Nobody is certain whether saying it or spelling it is harder, but you can buy especially long envelopes for sending things there.

Scrabble

There is nothing like a good game of Scrabble when you are feeling wild, especially when it is accompanied by hot cocoa. Quite similar to a crossword, it was invented in 1931 by one Alfred M. Butts, a New York architect, who called it Criss Cross. The game was renamed Scrabble and came to prominence under James Brunot, who bought the manufacturing rights from Butts. It has become a worldwide hit and you can take part in international tournaments as well as play it on the Internet. The highest recorded score was by a carpenter in Massachusetts called Michael Cresta in 2006, who accumulated 830 points. Words you should keep in mind next time you play include:

Words using Q:

- Bezique – a French card game, believed to have migrated from Spain.
- Qat – also spelled 'kat' or 'khat'. It's a plant you chew for a mildly narcotic effect. Try it with your daffodils.

- Qetzal – a Central American bird with a long tail.
- Quixotic – extravagantly chivalrous or generous – except when losing at Scrabble.
- Squeezy – like your loved one after too much nougat.

No vowels but using Y:

- Crypt – a space below a church where you might have ended up being stored in olden times.
- Flysch – a series of sediments featuring marine deposits like clay and shale. Isn't shale a lovely word?
- Nymphs – the ancient Greeks thought they were female spirits who guarded woods and rivers. They didn't have cheerleaders back then.
- Tryst – meeting between lovers, especially a secretive one involving hanky-panky.
- Xylyl – to do with Xylene, which is an isometric mixture of other things. Go and look it up – you need the exercise.

No vowels and not using Y:

- Brr – code for 'I am cold. Can we stop sitting behind a windbreak on the beach in March pretending we are having fun and go home?', and good for starting arguments about whether it is allowed in Scrabble, too.

- Crwth – an ancient Celtic stringed instrument, a bit like a cithara.
- Hmm – the noise you made when your children wanted to borrow the car.
- Nth – an adjective describing the position of a subject in a sequence; i.e. to the nth degree.
- Psst – a noise you make to get someone's attention. Or a slow fart. Both can have the same effect but the response varies.

Bridge

They say the difference between a demented maniac hell-bent on hurting people with an axe and a bridge partner is you can talk things over with the maniac. The occasional fraught scene aside, bridge is brilliant for meeting people and having fun. It's also very good for your mind. As the grey matter becomes less elastic and learning new tricks grows harder, it is advantageous to start playing bridge in your fifties so that by the time you are in your sixties or seventies, you know what's going on and can hold your own. It's also a great way of getting out of the house if your day now revolves around when the best-looking daytime television presenters are on air.

Derived from whist, bridge was invented towards the end of the nineteenth century. Rumours that the name actually came from the first bust-up between two bridge partners, where one of them was pushed off a nearby bridge to a dreadful ending, are unfounded. Contract bridge was dreamt up by Harold Stirling Vanderbilt in 1925 on a steamer en route from Los Angeles to Havana. Harold was also a rather fine yachtsman and won the America's Cup in 1930. He invented the first forcing club bidding system, and the Vanderbilt Trophy remains one of the top prizes in the game.

In a nutshell, bridge is a card game played by four players who team up to form two partnerships and involves varying degrees of skill and the presence of Lady Luck. The game is made up of the auction, which is called bidding, and play. When play is over you work out what your score is. If you are really bored by this point, take up nude skydiving instead. In a social context, people often play a few hands before or after a meal, making it a civilized occasion. Except when you get your rules muddled up, make a mistake and lose. Then you can expect harsh glares from your partner and being handed a macaroon with your cup of tea in a frosty manner.

Chapter Three

Keep on Trucking

There is another way to keep busy. If the idea of retirement has you reaching for the panic button (usually bought from the back of magazines, these conveniently hang on a piece of string around your neck), simply don't retire. As the baby boomer generation hurtles towards retirement, a gap is developing. While the number of people aged 55 to 64 in the UK will fall, the number of over-65s grows steadily like a greyish, wobbly mass. And this means that a high proportion of old-timers will opt to work on into their twilight years. You will be financially better off than many of your peers and you will keep mind and body stimulated and entertained. You will also be part of a swelling army of senior workers, increasingly valued for their broad experience and knack for making a decent hot beverage. Just over 30 per cent of the UK's working population is over 50, and in ten years this will have risen to around 40 per cent. The government is keen to do something for once too. Have a look at www.dwp.gov.uk. You might also try www.wrinklies.org (slogan: 'Been there, done that, got the cardigan'). From senior telemarketers to quantity surveyors, it's all out there. Just don't turn up for an interview with string holding up your trousers.

Jobs that laugh in the face of ageism

Consultant or trainer

Your long working years have left you with a wealth of expertise, and there are plenty of companies who will snap you up to train their staff. There is also a growing market in MBA colleges that actively recruit veterans from various industries to teach others by drawing on their time at the coalface. The great advantage is that if people start sniggering at the back of the class when you send your Powerpoint demonstration into meltdown by pressing the wrong thing, you can bark at them to shut up and they will take you seriously. Nobody fools with someone who might have fought in a war. There are secondary school teachers up and down the country who would give anything for that kind of respect.

Van washer

The exact age of Londoner Buster Martin is uncertain. Theories abound that he is 101, 94 or somewhere in between. He certainly isn't 23, anyway. Born in France, he went to a Cornish orphanage aged three and got his nickname when he thumped a priest on the nose. According to him, after spells working in the army and at Brixton Market and retiring at the tender age of 97, he got bored and restless and joined Pimlico Plumbers, washing their fleet of vans for a living. In 2008, Buster completed the London Marathon accompanied by two personal trainers and raised over £20,000 for charity. He said afterwards that he could have done it in much less than the ten hours it took him if it wasn't for his beer and fag breaks.

There has been official controversy about his exact age, and because of this he is not in the *Guinness World Records* book as the oldest Marathon runner, which instead went to Dimitrion Yordanidis, who completed a marathon in Athens at the sprightly age of 98. But Buster isn't exactly fazed about the Guinness people and their records. He once said, 'The only Guinness I am interested in is one I can drink.'

Charity shop assistant

OK, so it doesn't pay the bills, but you get first dibs on any items you want to snaffle for yourself, get to gossip all day with like-minded souls full of tales of red-hot scandal from their portrait painting evening class, and it bolsters your odds of getting into heaven. The downside is you have to rifle through bags of rags reeking of mothballs and try to play Connect Four with Monopoly pieces on quiet days – which is enough to drive you mad.

Acting extras

There are numerous agencies that specialise in the more mature actors and television and film are the favoured haunts of some of our most revered older thespians – though we are talking about extras, not leading roles. It's one in the eye for stick-thin actors making themselves sick after every meal or dieting by using drugs. You are mature enough not to care what the casting director thinks of your love handles, and you had to stop that cocaine habit years ago due to a dicky heart. The other great advantage is being part of the luvvie community. Old hands have unique stories to tell, and most of them are pretty mad so you will fit right in. You might not get paid very well, and will do hours of standing about, but the hot drinks are on tap and the scope for pointless chit-chat is endless.

A good example of a programme to aim for is *Miss Marple*. A beacon of hope where all around are losing their minds, she finds clues and solves murders like a well-matured dervish in an idyllic English setting – idyllic, except for the poor swine with the ice pick sticking out of them. It was the US that first gave her an airing on television in 1956, and the UK didn't cotton on to this powerful combination of wearing tweed and doing a bit of gardening until 1984. Being innovative types, the Japanese dreamt up an animated version that saw both Hercule Poirot and Miss Marple teaming up in a double whammy of crime solving. The best way to get in on the action is to find an agent or ring the producer and cajole them until their ears bleed.

Porn star

Possibly not for everyone, but the porn industry is happy for you to keep working well into your dotage. It's a case of putting your boots up in the air instead of hanging them up completely. Forget those honed and toned slim young things banging away at each other – the emerging market is letting it all hang out, wrinkles and all, with a bit of granny porn. From the respectful-sounding 'mature ladies' to a lot worse, quite who is into this is unclear, but there is certainly a wide enough DVD and Internet presence to make it worth looking out for current vacancies in your local paper. Storylines can also involve completely new angles. Where once a slim blonde gets the plumber round, now it's all about having your bus pass revoked for bad behaviour on the number 57 and having to go down to the local council office for a good spanking.

Chapter Four

Forty Winks

Also known as the catnap, siesta, doze, snooze or power nap, a quick bit of shut-eye is a formidable way of reviving yourself during the day. It also becomes a fact of life in later years as any kind of relaxing, be it with a book, the television or just thinking of nothing in a comfy chair for five minutes means you lose consciousness. It is believed that the idea of forty winks started a long time ago, when the first human beings who hadn't slept for a week got so irritated they couldn't get the espresso machine to work that they nearly beat each other senseless with animal bones. Ever since, sleep has been an important part of our lives.

The good news is that a six-year Greek study recently concluded that regular siestas reduce your chances of dying of heart disease by 34 per cent. Across the Mediterranean, low instances of heart disease are associated with a daily lie-down, although it has also been said that in some countries such as France the siesta is just an elaborate excuse for a bit of nooky, which also helps keep you perky. Researchers in the US found that it actually sharpened your mental faculties, once you had come round sufficiently to remember where on earth you were.

Armed with these statistics, when you are next criticised for dozing off, trot this one out to the over-stressed relatives around you, pointing to their hearts and muttering quietly, 'I give you five years.' They will soon come round to your way of thinking. Whoever coined the phrase 'You snooze, you lose' was a complete idiot.

The best of the rest

The afternoon doze

This is a classic entry-level nap for beginners – tactics range from donning an airline eye-mask and just passing out in your chair to a full-blown sleep in bed.

Evening television

Maybe it is because the other half wants to watch Alan Titchmarsh molesting some seagulls but, belly swelled with supper, all those exciting nuggets you highlighted in the *Radio Times* are soon distant trivialities in the land of nod.

The holiday siesta

The Spanish word *siesta* is derived from the Latin *sexta hora*, or 'sixth hour' – six hours after daybreak is midday, when everyone has a big lunch and a glass or two of Rioja followed by a cheeky kip. Often northern Europeans become converts to the siesta after Mediterranean holidays, where reading a book for five minutes before slumping into the happy abyss is all part of the package.

The summer hammock

If you have a garden and some conveniently placed trees, hang up a hammock. It might be the only sort of swinging you do these days, but it's germ-free and easier on the knees.

Christmas Day

Christmas would not be the same without granny making bad smells and grandpa asleep in a chair after one too many sherries. But a quick doze, real or faked, is a fabulous way of dodging the washing-up, side-stepping any family rows that have been simmering dangerously in the wings, and getting out of having to entertain the grandchildren, who lost their appeal shortly after the Queen's Speech when they laughed at your paper crown and then pulled your ears.

Wedding parties

This is actually more of a drunken stupor and the difference is you will wake up confused and belligerent rather than revitalised and alert. Blame will start to be distributed among the younger folk who were meant to be in charge of you, focusing on why you weren't taken home just after the cake was savaged with knives, and who allowed you to drink so much champagne anyway? If you want to be excluded from any future nuptials, pinch a few bums and make a lunging attempt to snog someone as you are steered across the dance floor and into a taxi. The wedding invitations will mysteriously dry up.

Three features of 'Tired nature's sweet restorer':

1. **The football dribble** – it's a classic move, sometimes accompanied by football on the TV after lunch. It is also guaranteed to scare people around you. Along with a few snuffles and snorts, a bit of dribble is a good sign – you were

so out of it you didn't care. Letting go of other bodily fluids is not recommended unless it's a tactical ploy to clear the house of unwanted guests.

2. The neck crack – the beauty of having a husband, wife or lover is that as you start to drift off, they will lovingly position a cushion behind your head, preventing you violently jerking your brain about, getting whiplash and forgetting how to spell Tuesday.

3. The death gasp – while experiencing particularly vivid dreams, you might let out an almighty gasp, seemingly your last, and panic everyone in the room into thinking you are on the verge of dying. If your children are desperately trying to get you to sign a hastily revised will as you come round, slap the vultures away with a rolled-up newspaper or bite them if they are within range.

Chapter Five

Pimp Your Ride

Many of us have heard music blaring, tyres screeching and girls with nothing but excessive drinking and cheap sex on their minds shrieking their heads off on a Saturday night – and that's just down at the local Women's Institute. Boy racers congregating in car parks to talk alloys and burn some rubber has become a national pastime in certain parts of the world, developing into a kind of motorised soundtrack to some old folks' lives if they are unlucky enough to live nearby. It's time to fight fire with fire and reclaim the streets with your customised electric scooter – just remember to indicate sensibly.

Wild guesswork estimates there are some 105,000 electric scooter users in the UK, with the worst of them earning the nickname 'Hell's Grannies'. Stories of dotty old riders in matching leather jackets rough-housing service stations, drinking too much sherry and having running battles with the police are unconfirmed. But what is known is that every year several of these hellraisers die and many are involved in incidents which end in tears. There was even the case of a woman accidentally reversing her scooter off a pier into the sea, which goes to show that you need to know what you are doing when it comes to this form of transport.

The vehicle

Things have come a long way since the first popular wheelchairs. Wicker bath chairs were the forerunners of the modern wheelchair and took their name from the city of Bath, where invalids were pushed about in their hooded contraptions. They were especially common in the 1830s. Modern scooters are self-propelled, strong, lightweight creations built to withstand even the most challenging situations, like joyriding up onto the kerb and ram-raiding Tesco. Typically they are three- or four-wheeled, with a natty mesh basket on the front for carrying the shopping or husband.

Examples include the Shoprider Altea 3 Portable Mobility Scooter, a three-wheeled design which can reach speeds of 4 mph and has the option of an oxygen bottle holder for the die-hard enthusiast. You can get eight miles out of it, and the simple lift-off battery-pack design means if you are doing gruelling 24-hour Le Mans-style endurance racing, battery changes in the pit lane are a doddle. The tyres are puncture proof, which is essential for urban tracks where broken lager bottles can be a hazard. At the other end of the scale, the Pride Celebrity X Sport reaches an underpant-destroying 8 mph. It can go for 25 miles on one charge, meaning you might be able to visit nearby relatives, and it has front and rear suspension for when you mount the pavement, scattering terrified pedestrians before you.

Accessorise

1. Lower the body – while perfect for the boy racer who owns a 1.3-litre Ford Escort, for you it will mean dropping your already low vehicle completely onto the tarmac. You might make an impressive grinding noise and there may even be some sparks but this will trash your ride in minutes, if it gets moving at all. Avoid.

2. Attach whale tails – those monstrous sculpted fins that go on the back are a bit passé now but they will still get them talking down at the bingo. Big body kits involving side skirts, rear skirts and bumpers are a better option, but doing it yourself with cardboard and sticky tape will detract from the overall effect. Find a local mechanic with a sense of adventure.

3. Add a front spoiler – a total pain when driving over speed bumps, but excellent for gathering small children and empty crisp packets.

4. Fit a huge exhaust – it's pointless on something that is electric-powered but, er, that's the point, innit?

5. Make your handlebars bristle with mirrors – see the cult film *Quadrophenia* for inspiration. At least five per handlebar are needed. The disadvantage is that if you get chased by hoodies or the police, you will see in your multiple mirrors far more people than there actually are, causing yourself unnecessary terror.

6. Slap on bumper stickers – with classic one-liners such as: 'Honk if you medicate' and 'Geriatrics do it standing up if someone supports them'.

7. Attach an aerial topped with a racoon tail – the fluffier the better. If this is hard to come by, find a dead fox or use the cat.

8. Add a federation flag sticker to the bonnet – *Dukes of Hazzard* meets 'peers with pensions'. If you are a man, it's perfectly all right to get your wife or girlfriend to cram herself into a tiny pair of denim shorts and call her Daisy.

Get the look

1. Get a white baseball cap – most high street sports shops can help.

2. Have a cigarette hanging from your mouth – ignore the health implications. Who cares at your age? Image is everything.

3. Get tattoos – designs of bulldogs, anchors and forces' sweetheart Vera Lynn are all acceptable. If you have a tattoo with the word 'Mum' below it, get this enlarged to 'Grandmum' – if she is somehow still around and you have enough excess flesh to do it. Or have go-faster flames tattooed on your bingo wings – the flabby undersides of your arms.

4. Invest in a scooter cape – a magnificent waterproof sheet for draping over you and your machine in adverse weather conditions. However, it is a huge fire hazard with that dangling cigarette, and your new boy racer friends won't want to hang out with a giant condom on four pram wheels – think pimp, not blimp.

Talk the talk

You need to know the lingo if you are going to rub shoulders with equally deranged delinquents:

Big bore

Don't worry, your new chavvy friends haven't heard about your trainspotting scrapbook from 1963. It refers to a wide exhaust pipe.

ICE

This is in-car entertainment, and includes sub-woofers, other speakers and DVD players. While hormone-crazed teenagers cornering on two wheels at 60 mph might have difficulty watching movies, your 4-mph scooter is ideally set up for this. Just don't let the police find you casting an eye over *Inspector Morse* while you're tearing up the tarmac.

Bad boy bonnet

This is a special bonnet that slants down and partially covers the headlights, giving the car a sleepy expression which is inexplicably appealing to boy racers. Your vehicle does not need to look any sleepier.

Flamer kit

This is a kit that you attach to your exhaust. It ignites unburned fuel that passes through the exhaust, usually after you have flicked a switch, shooting great big flames out of the back.

The only slight problem is your wagon is electric. A cheap alternative is to pick up a flamethrower left over from the war and hook it up to the back of your ride. Then get someone you aren't fond of to try it out for the first time – and don't wear anything flammable.

Shed

This is a badly modified or plain awful car. Do not get mixed up and start telling your new tracksuited friends about the contraption at the bottom of your garden or the best month to start planting tomatoes. Do tell them about your porn collection hidden there.

Win prizes

If you want to be the best and leave everyone else at the lights, techniques to hone include:

Left-foot braking

Common in motor racing; instead of using your right foot to brake, switch to your left. This means you are saving time by only using the right foot to accelerate.

Finding the optimum racing line

Don't be clever and point out that the fastest way to get somewhere is in a straight line. As you screech and skid around the car park, the racing line is the fastest way to get around a corner or series of corners, meaning that you glide around while losing as little speed as possible.

Minimising turbo-lag
This is the delay between pushing down the accelerator and when the turbo comes into effect.

Note: absolutely none of these apply to a motorised wheelchair, whose maximum speed is the same as a growing mushroom. But you can have an immense amount of pointless, expensive fun trying.

Driving for the hard of remembering

Elderly drivers sometimes get quite a bit of flak from young types who think they are cluttering up the roads unnecessarily. In Tokyo, the authorities are encouraging drivers over 65 to hand in their licences and stop snarling up an already chaotic traffic situation by offering incentives and savings. In 2007, there were 1.5 million drivers in the UK over the age of 75, which equates to a great deal of people peering intently ahead and accidentally retuning the radio while trying to operate the windscreen wipers. Driving has changed beyond all recognition in the last few decades, and you need to be aware of certain things:

1. The Highway Code was not invented at Bletchley Park and has nothing to do with the Enigma machine and World War Two. And it certainly wasn't a set of guidelines drawn up to keep Dick Turpin in check. That was the Highwayman Code.

2. When it's foggy, your husband or wife does not have to get out and walk in front of the car with a lantern – find the fog lights switch.

3. Unless you drive a Ford Prefect, which was invented before seat belts (but has lovely, springy seats, like the Citroën 2CV), you need to put one on. Also, let's get one thing clear; there are times when 'Belt up, dear' means put one on, and others when it means 'Will you just shut up for five minutes?'.

4. Do not go at 20 mph on the motorway. Not only do most other people have a lot of work and chores to do in any given day, which you are now ruining their chances of achieving, but odds are someone will plough into the back of you, scattering the parking money in the ashtray and decapitating the nodding dog on the parcel shelf.

5. Do not flee the scene of an accident – unless you want to keep your licence.

Alternatives to motoring

When you get slapped with an ASBO and barred from the car park, try the following electric-powered activities instead:

Wheelchair soccer

Played on a modified basketball court, either in motorised or manual wheelchairs, this is a physically demanding sport and shouldn't be attempted unless you know you can hold down ten pints and a chicken vindaloo afterwards.

Drag racing

This is just like racing in those needle-sharp machines of death that spout flames and reach speeds of 330 mph in less than five seconds – only with less call for parachutes to slow you down safely at the end. All you need is a nice, quiet cul-de-sac where you can bomb along in a straight line on your scooter. In the past, Hell's Grandpas have had the wrong idea about this event and turned up in fishnets and their best floral print frock with matching rouge. Don't.

The stair chair

Once you have got the hang of pimping your electric scooter, your new-found skill for adding on fins and spoilers can be applied to a stairlift to brighten up the ride. Obviously, only half of it can be pimped with a body kit as the rest is attached to the building, and tread carefully with speccing up the engine or you might end up putting yourself through a wall. Useful tail stickers include: 'This one goes all the way to heaven' and 'Seniors do it slowly'.

The electric chair

Not the kind that causes your eyeballs to pop out, although this is always a risk when you see the price tag in the shop. This is the sort that goes in the sitting room and can be electronically adjusted to facilitate standing up or releasing trapped wind. There are also additional dangers after you have brought home one of these huge, but useful, items of furniture and are fiddling with the remote controls and wondering if it can switch on your electric blanket in the bedroom. Do be aware that this is a serious piece of kit and, if handled inappropriately or under the influence of Night Nurse, you could well hurl yourself across the room to an untimely demise and a humorous eulogy.

Chapter Six

Fashion

You know you are approaching the autumnal era when you are receiving hand-me-ups instead of hand-me-downs, as your fashion-savvy children take pity on your ailing wardrobe. But the great thing is you have arrived at a point in your life where you have realised that materialism is shallow. The fact that materialism is also an expensive habit you can't afford is irrelevant. Second-hand sweatshirts promoting obscure university basketball teams from the American Midwest or declaring 'Benidorm Does It Better' are all fair game now. The important thing is it cost nothing and doesn't divert funds from important stuff like cigarettes and Scotch. You are now a champion of recycling rather than a carbon-belching consumer.

The balance of years has shifted when you find yourself shopping for more things by telephone or Internet than on the high street. Charity shops remain a good source of raiment on the cheap and are rich hunting grounds for a bit of conversation with like-minded souls if you are bored with your lot and need to moan with someone about the state of the country today. But sartorial elegance has its triumphs and pitfalls for the old-timer, and you don't want to be the scruffy one at the bus stop with the holey shoes that are more pavement than patent. Let's start at the top and work our way down.

Hats

From the time when our prehistoric ancestors saw it was raining outside and decided to pull half a rabbit over their heads before venturing out, hats have been a personal statement about who you are. They denoted your status in society or identified who could give you the biggest bollocking in the military. From the straw ones first seen in early Egyptian paintings to the white baseball cap of boy racers, hats speak a language that even the hard of hearing can tune into.

Nowadays, hats are one area where the older generation often still has the upper hand. Young women might be slim and savvy but they can look a bit daft in a trilby – private-investigator-meets-cross-dressing-lesbian, served with a slice of ego and finished with a dash of nonsense. Even celebrities like the model Kate Moss can't pull it off. They rightfully belong on the heads of coffin-dodgers, and it's fair play to have an old codger's gripe about this fact. Flat caps are also far more distinguished atop a bit of grey and look downright pretentious on Prince William, who needs to add at least a decade before the overall image can be taken seriously. There are plenty of different models to choose from. The bucket hat is ideal for fishing or sailing and the Akubra, the wide Australian hat for keeping the sun off and beating back deadly snakes, will lend you the air of an exotic explorer from distant climes who has just dropped by for a quick game of rummy and a cup of Earl Grey. The beret will mark you out as a learned Francophile with an unhealthy interest in red wine and the Dordogne. The panama, from Ecuador, is essential for high-end social events like the cricket at Lords or anything where a picnic and opera collide.

Ladies at the turn of the twentieth century would have had to change hats several times during the day, depending on the task at hand. Stick to a few good ones for minimising faff and storage space. The Queen leads the way in fancy headgear. Remember that black felt tricorn with scarlet plumes that she wore for her first trooping the colour in 1951? It was daring and flamboyant and made several onlookers grow woozy with excitement.

When life is starting to pass you by and younger people act like you don't exist, nothing beats a marvellous hat for giving a royal wave to onlookers as you are rounded up and driven back to the home by white-coated staff. Try it. People will soon be taking pictures on their mobile phones just in case you really *are* the Queen. Also, do not forget to use a couple of hatpins – she has not lost a hat in bad weather to this day. The plastic rain hood is another classic style favoured by the senior citizen, although this leans more on the side of practicality while gently killing any fashion sense with a large serrated knife.

Hair today, gone tomorrow

Grey hair appears when the hair follicles are no longer producing as much pigment, which means your hair gradually turns colourless. It is also a wonderful leveller. You might cheat with dye but nearly everyone goes grey or white in the end. However, there are a few hairstyles to choose from as you age:

Totally bald

A simple and total reduction means you save about an hour a day on messing about in front of the mirror primping and styling. Use this extra time to heckle the Salvation Army Band in the local shopping centre when they get a note wrong.

The comb-over

Accompanied by sniggering and pointing wherever it goes, if your old friend Bob starts turning up at the working men's club with one of these, for pity's sake tell him to behave and cut it off.

The bouffant

Using back-combing and hair spray, you can soon have the coiffured allure of Hyacinth Bucket from *Keeping up Appearances* or the steely persona of Margaret Thatcher. Kim Jong-il, the not so 'Dear Leader' of North Korea, might be a brute but he's got a comical version of this hairstyle.

BALD   COMB-OVER   BOUFFANT

The ponytail

Having a shiny grey ponytail is best reserved for fashion designers, folk musicians, ageing hippies who grow their own and former playboys who can't let go of their youth.

The wig

Spend a bit extra on a decent one or you will look like you are being ridden by a badger. Also, be wary of street urchins who might steal it as part of an elaborate process of joining a less violent inner-city gang.

The Gatsby

The Great Gatsby is set in the Jazz Age of the 1920s. The film of the 1925 novel by F. Scott Fitzgerald shows the clean, swept-back style worn by gentlemen, with a side-parting so sharp you could slice ham with it. It's a classic to wow the ladies with.

The slick back

This uses obscure hair products like hair oil, a substance only found on a dusty shelf in those barbershops that still have a stripy pole. Men will remember that their father was working this look in the 1920s; a classic style with a certain appeal, mainly to gangsters in pinstriped suits and small, winged insects that became stuck in it.

The purple rinse

Here's one for the ladies. Though it's considered a style icon of the past, this vivid creation can still occasionally be found nodding from Bognor to Torquay. The culprit who went and invented the blue rinse has never been caught. Avoid unless you are happy to join those that live beyond the fringes of the fashionable world.

Wonderwear

Look in the back of any national magazine or paper and you will find thousands of adverts for the kind of women's underwear that, at first glance, might appear to be something skydivers would use to safely reach the ground. With wild promises, from holding in your flabby tummy to guaranteeing you get the best table in fine restaurants, this is a multi-million pound industry. Young people are at once fascinated and terrified by these alien adverts for unseen garments. What does this strap do? Where does that go? And why is it all so large? Don't worry – they will understand some day. Examples can be viewed on: www.rigbyandpeller.com or www.themagicknickershop.co.uk. And be aware that beige is not always best.

Control underwear

Not the kinky leather sort for when he's been a very naughty boy – these garments are made to hold in and flatten those unwanted spare tyres. Body stockings can help keep everything trim from bust to bottom. Essentially, it's like squeezing a seamless, flesh-coloured bag into a smaller, seamless, flesh-coloured bag. Ranging from pants to corsets, this concept is a brilliant way of looking like you have been exercising and dieting – until someone gets you naked.

If you are a traditionalist, you might also have a girdle lurking in your closet. Historically, it began life as a belt which showed less of your tackle than the troublesome loincloth. The modern version, which is free from bones and comfortably elasticated, replaced corsets in mainstream fashion in the 1920s. Gradually superseded by lighter, slightly more attractive garments, they have fallen from favour since the 1970s. The best use for them today is as a safety harness for cleaning the upstairs windows.

Front-fastening bras

Although the man of the house might miss a good fumble around the back, as his fingers start to work less well a front-fastening bra can be a good idea if you don't want to be waiting so long for him to get it undone that you fall asleep.

Skirts

Despite their outwardly feminine and unthreatening appearance, skirts have certain dangerous aspects to them:

1. Less is not always more. If you find yourself in a demure A-line with a sensible hemline, quietly congratulate yourself on having a degree of modesty and decorum. If you find yourself in a miniskirt ordering a 'sex on the beach' in a nightclub at 3 a.m., it is time to have a quiet word with yourself.

2. If you wear Harris tweed and go exploring the countryside in winter, you might unexpectedly have a shotgun thrust in your hands and be told to blast pheasants from the heavens by a ruddy-cheeked stranger. On the plus side, there will be a hot meal and booze afterwards.

3. If you are in a library and your polyester skirt with matching jacket is rustling excessively, you will be told to pipe down by someone in comfortable shoes.

4. If you are a man and you aren't Scottish, Balinese or Eddie Izzard, you shouldn't be wearing one – at least not in the open.

Other fashions to avoid:

1. Miniskirts. Just admit it – varicose veins are not the height of sexiness.

2. Micro bikinis – no, no, no, no and no.

3. Tops with plunging necklines that reveal most of your cleavage – age like a fine wine, not a bottle of alcopop.

4. Baseball caps worn backwards – unless you are thrashing your pimped electric scooter around a car park.

5. Long beige raincoats that flashers wear – especially if you are already a flasher. Break the mould.

Footwear

Sensible shoes

This is the border-crossing where fashion is handed over in exchange for practicality. You might not look very sexy but you will be steady on your feet in adverse conditions. Invariably, they will have easy-access Velcro straps or be slip-ons for speedy getaways. They will have good, grippy soles with plenty of durability for all those long treks to the corner shop. They may well have come from a magazine. Things they will not have include flashing lights, compartments of clear gel or small pumps so you can inflate the shoes around your foot for a snug fit.

Sandals

Rumour has it that these were first called Jesus sandals after someone shouted 'Jesus! Look at those awful sandals.' You will look like a Geography teacher, although they will allow your stifled trotters to breathe more easily. The main disadvantage is that if you have yellowing or rotten toenails, a month of fluff between your toes or really bulging veins, it will all be in the public domain.

Good for the sole – slippers explored and explained

These are such an integral part of the old-timer's existence, they need a section all to themselves. You had them as a child, you might have kept a pair through your summer years, but sure as eggs is eggs, we all end up in slippers in our dotage. Slippers are one of the true delights of getting on in life, a tartan comfort blanket lovingly enveloping each foot in artificial warmth and rubberised grip.

You know you have really arrived when you find yourself in the high street buying the paper in your latest low-heeled M&S numbers, looked at in horror by secretly envious youngsters, who have to go through a torturous and expensive process of choosing fashionable footwear. You can save yourself enough time getting ready in the morning to quickly nip in the bookies and plonk a tenner on Joe Lively in the 1.05 at Cheltenham. You will also be left alone by hoodies as there is a hint of recklessness about someone who wears their slippers in the street. You might have wandered out of an old people's home and be dangerously low on medication. Some of them might have even got the slipper as a child and may regard yours with an old and dreadful tingle in their buttocks.

Slippers, like women binding their feet, seem to have originated in Asia and there are mentions of them in use in China from the twelfth century. Early versions were similar to flip-flops, with leather soles and a piece of wood which went between the toes. People in India were also documented as wearing embroidered ones and others which curled up at the end and being quite cheerful about it.

Because of their custom of removing shoes before entering the home, the Japanese always don slippers to slop about in indoors, saving the parquet flooring from getting scratched. For foreign traders baffled by this footwear fetish, at the end of the nineteenth century the Japanese hit upon the great idea of slippers that could fit over normal shoes. They made you feel like you had leprosy or were entering a chemical weapons factory, but at least they gave everyone something to point at and laugh about. These kinds of slippers still feature in modern Japanese life, along with toilet slippers, which should only be worn in the thunderbox. If your hosts find you trampolining on their bed while still wearing the toilet slippers after a visit to the bathroom, they will ask you to leave.

In the West, carpet slippers are mainly worn in the house of an evening. 'Pipe and slippers' became a common phrase describing a homely scene – the man by the fire, smoking a pipe and relaxing in his favourite footwear after a hard day's work while the wife fiddled about in the kitchen. Nowadays it is used by the young to be rude about staid domestic types who are past it. If this is used to refer to you, clip whoever said it round the ear at once.

Styles and prices now cover a wide spectrum, from ones down the market saying 'Sex Machine' in red letters for £1.99 to Ted Baker's suede offerings at over £30. If you are not yet ready for slippers, Crocs or flip-flops can break you in gently and Ugg boots can get you used to that sheepskin and suede feel, which makes certain people claustrophobic at first. Technology lovers might like to purchase microwavable slippers, which come out warm and scented. You might not want to eat anything else that comes out of the microwave for the next week, but going hungry is a small price to pay for lavender-scented toes.

Five easy ways to get them on

1. Your partner – it's not a glamorous job but it's a long way to bend down and besides, you have to put up with their over-boiled sprouts and obsession with programmes about decorating the house, so it's the least they can do.

2. The dog – the really savvy old-timer not only trains the dog to fetch their slippers, but gets the beast to stand there and act as a support as they pull them on. This is best suited to sturdy working dogs – small, yappy specimens are utterly useless, although we knew this already. Also, be careful with puppies, as they will shred your favourite pair in seconds.

3. The grandchildren – some say it's child labour, but it's about time they made themselves useful when they visit.

4. A long-handled shoehorn – as mentioned in Chapter One, they sell for around £4 (try www.helptheagedshop.co.uk for starters) and are lifesaving devices. Also doubles as a whacking stick for chasing cats out of the garden while shouting 'Bastards!' at the cats/neighbours/anyone who will listen.

5. Jehovah's Witnesses – if they want you to be saved, you aren't doing it without your best moccasins.

Foot facts

- There is a hip hop producer called DJ House Shoes, who operates out of Detroit.

- The Pope wears Prada – rumours were rife that Pope Benedict XVI's slippers were made by the luxury Italian brand, but the Vatican has revealed that they were made by his own humble cobbler.

- Another type of slipper is a man who, while coursing for hares, slips dogs off their leads so they can have great fun chasing the hares. He might well occupy a corner seat in his local pub and doesn't like his pint being fooled with. Do not play cards with this man.

- The showy lady's slipper, from the lady's slipper family of orchids, is the state flower of Minnesota.

- Arguably the most famous pair of slippers (although they were actually shoes) were Dorothy's ruby ones in *The Wizard of Oz*. Note that trying to get out of the ironing does not work if you click your heels together. Chances are you don't own a pair anyway. One of the five pairs made for the film sold for $666,000 in 2000, and most state pensions don't quite stretch to that.

Chapter Seven

Entertainment

Ever since Socrates was having a slow day and thought he would keep himself amused by having a think about ethics, people have needed to keep themselves entertained. And old-timers are no different. Whether it's vehemently defending your pruning techniques or wondering who you can ring up and shout at, stave off boredom by going out and seizing the world by the scruff of its neck. Or stay at home and peer at the neighbours through your net curtains. The good thing about seniority is nobody can tell you what to do.

Films you probably won't enjoy very much

Going to the cinema or renting a DVD is now more popular than ever, and still costs less than two or three pints down the Red Lion. But there are certain films out there that just won't be your cup of lapsang souchong. Save yourself the effort of renting these very loud, chaotic options with our cinematic guide:

Bulletproof Monk

A monk and a pickpocket combine forces to battle with loads of people over an ancient scroll – loads of great martial arts and nothing philosophical whatsoever to consider. It will leave you with a vague headache and a mild sense of 'What?'

Die Another Day

After being incarcerated and doing very little shopping in North Korea, James Bond does battle with a few baddies and ends up at an ice palace that gets melted by a big thing that harnesses the rays of the sun and threatens the future of the world. It's packed with guns, cars, cars with guns and ice – and lots of noise. The actress Rosamund Pike isn't unattractive, however.

Con Air

A bunch of maximum security prisoners breaks free while in transit on a plane that makes Alitalia look organised. It contains violence, baggage moving around in the overhead lockers during the flight and absolutely no peanuts – most unsettling.

Silent Hill

A deeply unpleasant, creepy horror which veers from genuinely scary to the bit where the director might well have got bored, taken his girlfriend off to California for a spot of wine tourism and left the crew to just finish it without him. It's very loud, gory and daft.

Armageddon

Lots of asteroids fall to earth. Then NASA realises one really big one is going to crash straight into the planet, ruining everyone's plans to buy shoes this weekend at the very least. Astronauts are sent to blow it up by putting nuclear devices inside it, creating yet another hideous demonstration of American patriotism.

Harry Potter and the Chamber of Secrets

Hugely irritating teenage actors are joined by silly special effects and a plot that never requires you to exercise thought. It will leave you feeling mentally bereft and slightly fed up that you wasted 154 minutes of your precious life watching this when you could have been counting the spoons in the cutlery drawer or polishing the goldfish.

Five safe bets

1. On Golden Pond
2. Gone with the Wind
3. Casablanca
4. The Sound of Music
5. Driving Miss Daisy

How to get on the *Antiques Roadshow*

Your other half has found a chipped vase in a box in the attic and suddenly everyone is avidly discussing the Ming Dynasty around the house. Talk soon turns to getting on the *Antiques Roadshow*, that perennial Sunday evening favourite where the only thing that can get the blood pressure up is when Mrs Dawes from Darlington discovers her nineteenth-century microscope is worth more than her house. There are also versions of the programme in the US, Sweden and the Netherlands. One of the most expensive items to date was a series of 25 Filipino watercolours that turned up at an edition filmed in Brussels in 1995. They went on to fetch a cool £265,000 at auction. In the US, a Navajo blanket in Tucson in Arizona was valued between £176,000 and £251,000, which is a lot more than you paid for that thing wrapped round your knees. Check the BBC website (www.bbc.co.uk) for details of where the experts will be visiting and expect long queues, regional accents, flasks of tea and an almost risky level of jollity. You never know – that typewriter from the 1920s you picked up at the car boot sale might just pay for several new hips.

Five ways to beat the *Antiques Roadshow* queues

1. Sleep overnight in the car to be first in line. People already do this so you have to clandestinely superglue their car doors shut in the dead of night to beat the morning rush.

2. Study blueprints of the location and try to infiltrate the perimeter through the sewage system. People with special forces training are most suited to this.

3. Borrow a paramedic's uniform and a wheelchair and wheel a friend in, saying they can't stand in queues as they suffer from gerontophobia (a fear of growing old).

4. Feign illness and get real paramedics to wheel you in. You will have to get across the point that you don't want to go to the nearest hospital. They are trained to expect you to be difficult so you may have to insist that nothing will make you feel better than having your heirlooms fondled by strangers.

5. Fight with everything you have got to work your way to the front. Elbowing people and distracting them by talking about the weather are entirely within the rules.

A guide to curtain twitching

Much like lawn bowls or topiary, curtain twitching is the realm of the old-timer, and when there is less going on in your own life you naturally want to watch other people's. Net curtains, which allow light in but keep the gaze of nosy strangers out, are believed to have first twitched in England in the eighteenth century. The more expensive ones were even made of silk lace. These days the best way to safely observe events in your street is through a sturdy pair of net curtains and with a good, steady wrist. The key to really successful twitching is to subtly let the neighbours know you saw every bit of their blazing row. But it's important to remember those moments of extreme danger when you don't want to get caught twitching – typically when the TV licence inspector appears or that weirdly tall kid with the ginger hair from down the street is wandering past, discarding crisp packets with abandon. A sudden wrong twitch at such a critical juncture could well result in a brick through the window and your hand/curtain coordination would be damaged for weeks.

If you want to take your twitching seriously, keeping a logbook of goings-on or setting up your own video camera are unhealthy, obsessive practices but may be useful if you end up in court. If you never wash your net curtains and do a lot of deep fat frying, they may eventually become see-through and betray you when you are peering at the neighbours bringing home their new flat screen TV.

If you live in a windswept valley in the middle of nowhere, curtain twitching is pointless and faintly ludicrous. Also note that as you get older, you might accidentally find yourself openly staring at people from your front garden – remember that direct eye contact for anything more than a casual glance in rough neighbourhoods is flirting with hospital. There are three essential twitching techniques for people in urban or village settings:

The opener

Approach the left-hand side of the window, shielding yourself from sight using the wall, and gently lift the curtain with your right hand, raising it slightly and creating the ideal viewing gap. A common error is moving the curtain too fast (our eyes are attracted to movement) and accidentally dropping it, causing a tell-tale swish of material. You can approach the right-hand side of the window and simply use your left hand to gently part it from the frame. Being ambidextrous is vital in case you sustain a hand injury from a fall or playing too much Scrabble.

The midfield of vision

Evaluate your net worth by sending your wife, husband or a friend out to the driveway to test how see-through your curtains are. When you are confident you are invisible, you can safely approach the middle of the curtains, which gives you a much wider field of vision and the chance to subtly use the middle gap in the curtains for clandestine observation. You might also suffer having your cover blown when an unwitting relative switches on the light in the room you are twitching in, neatly silhouetting you for all to see. This is remedied with animated hisses and throwing something heavy at them.

The twitch-off

When you have become confident with the above techniques, it is time to go head to head with the neighbours opposite. This helps you to learn new tricks and build confidence, while asserting twitching authority in your street. The best method is to send a friend or partner outside to fiddle with the car aerial or check for lost mail, and wait by the window. When your neighbour gives the initial 'I might be interested' twitch, tug the curtain heavily twice to show them you are there and have seen them. Most will flee and go back to the television. If they do not leave, you will have to agitate the curtains with increasing force. There is a risk of thrashing the curtains around so much they come off the rails. If this happens, hide until nightfall and then move to another county.

Rumour-spreading for beginners

As things slow down in your own scandal department, it's time to start rummaging about in other people's. A verbal equivalent of curtain twitching, some top lines for getting a bit of trouble on the boil and keeping yourself entertained are:

- 'And I couldn't help noticing that Trevor from number fifty-six was putting what looked like a body in the boot of his car on Friday night.'

- 'Well, that's odd. She told me she hated Gladys's collection of humorous tea towels.'

- 'And you'll never guess who I saw buying condoms in Boots this morning – ribbed ones too.'

- 'They aren't going to Ethel's for Christmas because the dog is always humping the furniture. They have told her that they are in Kenya.'

- 'You only give your grandchildren twenty pounds each for Christmas? Well, maybe we are overdoing it with their holiday to Thailand.'

Swing a shoe

It's very fashionable and good for you to try your hand, or foot, at a bit of dancing. Ballroom dancing dates back to the eighteenth century when the upper classes would descend on spa towns like Bath to drink water that smelled of farts and do a polite minuet. But then those naughty Austrians brought over the Viennese waltz and it all went wrong. It even moved Sir Henry Englefield to write a poem castigating the waltz. Of course, he was a jealous type and an early critic of wife-swapping parties when people put the keys to their pony and trap in a bowl. Towards the end of the nineteenth century, seaside towns saw a boom in dancing. Polkas gave way to foxtrots, but the craze for ballroom dancing went into a decline, partly because of the hokey-cokey, which frankly has a lot to answer for. But ballroom is very much back in the limelight and tea dances are once again a going concern. Dancing today is social, healthy and a bit sexy (but well-behaved) – three winning reasons to love it. Tea dances, usually held in the afternoon or early evening, are often set to romantic music. To this day, the senior traveller still packs a case and heads to Blackpool, where the Tower Ballroom holds events throughout the summer. Tea dances are also popular in the US.

Knitting

For as long as there's been sheep that have let humans get close enough, there has been bestiality. But more worryingly, there has also been knitting. It is believed that knitting evolved from crochet or the repairing of fishing nets. Examples of crocheted clothes have been discovered in Egyptian tombs stretching back as far as the fourth century. They were believed to be unwanted socks a grandmother knitted for someone who later hid them and claimed the garments had shrunk in the Nile. In the sixteenth century, stockings were being made by hand but it was in the twentieth century that the arrival of the knitting machine made the whole laborious process a bit easier. You might be tempted to take up knitting using needles. The oversized jumpers you make will save a fortune on Christmas presents, until grandchildren are old enough to realise that a woolly hat is not the same as a Playstation. When you grow bored of making scarves, twenty alternative uses for knitting needles are:

1. Self-defence against intruders
2. Cleaning your ears (carefully)
3. Picking your nose (very carefully)
4. Opening the post
5. Viciously stabbing the post when it turns out to be nothing but brochures for life insurance
6. Poking trick-or-treaters through the letterbox
7. Changing channels on the television with minimal movement
8. Pointing at stuff when your laser pointer breaks down
9. Getting things from under a chair
10. Getting your husband or wife out of their chair
11. Performing affordable acupuncture on people you don't really like
12. Very large hairpins
13. Chopsticks for people with big hands
14. Reusable BBQ skewers
15. Staking out small plants
16. Playing mini-javelin in the garden
17. Warding off large dogs that are roaming your property
18. Harpooning the koi carp in your pond when you have had enough of them doing nothing but swimming about all day and demanding to be fed

19. Skewering the neighbour's cat after it peed in your pansies
20. Skewering the neighbour after they fail to grasp the importance of the pansies

Bingo

Mankind has always liked to have a bit of a gamble, from when cavemen used to slap sabre-toothed tigers on the bum and then run like mad. It is believed that the Italians were playing a game of chance loosely based on bingo in the fifteenth century. The French really got hold of the game in the eighteenth century and started using cards to mark the numbers and calling them out aloud to a captive audience. Germany used it to teach children how to count and spell, then an American called Edwin Lowe was said to have witnessed a game called Beano in Atlanta in the 1920s. When an enthusiastic player yelled out 'Bingo!' instead of 'Beano!', the name was born. Lowe was said to just be pleased that the same excitable person's earlier cry of 'wobbly bits' was largely ignored.

Also fetchingly known as housey-housey, bingo is one of the world's most popular and least expensive forms of gambling, making it an ideal hobby as you won't blow the money for the weekly shop. Having to listen to the caller announcing the numbers and ticking off the boxes is good for hand/eye coordination, and getting that winning line and shouting 'House!' really checks if those new, cheaper heart pills the NHS prescribed are working for you.

If you are something of a technophobe and have only just mastered the toaster, beware. Bingo is moving forward with the introduction of PET. These are programmable electronic tickets that allow you to play multiple tickets on a computerised touchpad, which is linked to the caller using wireless technology. If you didn't understand this last line, just stick to burning the crumpets.

Bingo lingo

Do not get your fat ladies muddled with your trombones when the numbers are being yelled out. Bingo calls that might leave the budding old-timer generally baffled include:

1 – Buttered scone. It was this sort of indulgence that caused the two fat ladies in the first place.

3 – I am free. I am sexually available. Note that sleeping with the bingo caller doesn't help you win.

4 – Bobby Moore. It is good to periodically remind ourselves of the 1966 World Cup that England somehow won – if only because it looks like being the only time.

5 – Man alive. Not if he has told the wife he isn't going to the bingo with her next week.

7 – God's in heaven. You hope. Or all that church was a total waste of time.

9 – Doctor's orders. Which are fun to ignore.

11 – Legs. They are lovely. Gets all the men stirred up.

17 – Often been kissed. True.

19 – Goodbye teens. Sad but true.

20 – Getting plenty. You would be surprised how many old-timers do.

26 – Bed and breakfast. Traditionally it would cost two and six – two shillings and six pence. Now it's £180 a night but you get biscuits.

29 – In your prime. If you are planning to live until you are 160 years old.

32 – Buckle my shoe. I can't reach.

35 – Flirty wives. They're hussies, the lot of them. It's just a question of finding them.

40 – Life begins at. Nonsense – it's 60.

44 – Droopy drawers. If the elastic is gone, they can end up round your ankles.

65 – Old age pension. It might just keep you in vodka.

78 – Heaven's gate. It's going to be locked and you have no idea where you hid the key.

81 – Fat lady and a little wee. One too many lagers in the break.

90 – End of the line. Time to take up extreme mountain biking.

Volunteer

As mentioned in Chapter Three, working in charity shops is one way of keeping yourself on the straight and narrow. Although, in your case it probably isn't straight and definitely isn't narrow. And this kind of work is the tip of the iceberg – organisations across the land are calling out for do-gooders who like to be bossy and can readily join others in a bit of chit-chat while buffing their halo. Options range from repairing drystone walls in Cumbria to stopping people from stealing priceless artefacts in a draughty castle in Wales. If you know how to creosote a fence or stop a hoodie from becoming a career criminal then stick up your hand. Or use it to type www.volunteering.org.uk and www.nationaltrust.org.uk.

Women's Institute

Not to be confused with the American state of Wisconsin, although both produce quite a bit of cheese. The WI has long been a refuge for ladies to get away for a bit of like-minded banter and charitable cake-baking. Started in 1915, it aimed to improve rural communities and get the ladies to help produce food during World War One. There are over 6,800 branches in the UK and they encompass many age groups, activities and hobbies, from cross stitch to tutting for beginners. However, it appears that the pressures of modern life have got in amongst scone-baking as well. Recent rumours suggest that WI members are buying produce and passing it off as their own. If this is you, just remember to put that loaf of bread in a plain paper bag or your ruse will unravel quicker than a badly made scarf. It is easy to find a WI near you – have a look at www.womens-institute.co.uk or, for the less technically minded, ask at the local jumble sale. Chief skills that are much sought after include:

1. Making really good jam

2. Getting your clothes off for charity calendars

3. Talking feverishly during coffee mornings

4. Having strong ideas on how to deal with local cowboys who are using high-pressure tactics over the telephone to sell walk-in baths

5. Listening to talks entitled 'Funny things that happened to me when I was a vicar' and not wanting to give the speaker a good kicking by the end of it

Chapter Eight

Striking Up Conversations With Complete Strangers

Old-timers are masters of communication when it comes to talking with strangers, partly because they are from a forgotten age when people were nice to each other, and partly because they only have a budgerigar to talk to at home. Classic settings for striking up conversations are:

The bus stop

A seemingly infinite number of combinations exist for chatting to other people waiting for the bus. Start cautiously with an enquiry about the route/time/bus number/when the last bus came through. People of a similar age or older are usually a safe bet. The young mostly get nervous and self-conscious and don't want their street cred to get dented. If your chosen conversationalist seems interested, move on to recent bus journeys (delays and mishaps are always popular topics) and then go for the heavier subjects, including the price of the bus and how the new seats are gentler on one's bottom.

Talking about the weather

A dependable option through the ages, the weather is the meadow upon which conversation with strangers has flourished. If it's pouring with rain this tends to start a conversation off gloomily but then it can either descend into outright complaining, which is always popular, or to 'Oh well, mustn't grumble', and further opportunities to show that you are an optimist. This can be especially useful if you fancy the person you are discussing global warming with. They do not want to make a date with a miserable doomsayer. There's *Grumpy Old Men* (or *Women*) on the television for that.

Minding your peas and queues

When standing in a supermarket queue, conversation can range from nutritional topics related to what the person behind or in front is purchasing, to what kind of loo paper is on a 'two for one' deal. Remember that talking so much that you are completely unprepared when the time comes to pay goes down very badly, especially when it's Saturday and working professionals in their thirties and forties are wondering why you couldn't have done all your shopping during the week. Actually, why couldn't you?

The lift

There is nothing like a captive audience, and if it is a hospital lift and there are any fit, healthy looking people there, corner them and show them your fresh scars and oozing wounds. They'll remember you, anyway.

Cultural events

You might be on one of those art trails where artists let you wander around their house, view their work and furtively see if they have done the washing-up. Or you could be nosing around in someone's garden on an open day while the owners look skyward and pray the crocuses don't get trampled on. Either way, you will probably be surrounded by similarly aged individuals and you are already united by a common interest. Stand in front of a particularly emotive painting, installation or flower arrangement and gently offer comments as bait to those lurking nearby. It's like shooting fish in a barrel, only crueller.

Chapter Nine

Gardening

Gardening is to the greys what not believing things is to Victor Meldrew. Not only is it a wonderful way of getting outdoors and giving yourself a dose of oxygen, but it will help with cardiovascular health and stamina. You can also burn 350 calories in an hour, which is handy if the only thing you are currently growing is fat.

The gardening workout

1. Hoeing – good for the upper body, especially those bingo wings.

2. Shovelling – this is essentially like weightlifting but without the intense monotony, and useful if you have murdered someone and need to hide the body.

3. Raking – this is actually similar to rowing but with significantly less chance of drowning, unless you trip over the gnome and land face first in the ornamental pond.

4. Mowing – pushing a heavy mower is like working out on a treadmill, and your calves will feel it. An alternative is training juvenile cows to cut the grass (commonly known as 'mooing') but it can take several weeks and they will wreck the foxgloves.

5. Pruning – good for strengthening your hands so that you can open jars and tins more easily, as well as grasping those annoying silver foil tops on plastic containers of milk rather than attacking them with scissors.

A gardener's paradise

The gazebo

It sounds like something wandering the plains of Tanzania, but the gazebo is an important place to go for a furtive cigarette or pipe when the weather is inclement. It can also make a wonderful Christmas grotto for the grandchildren. Dress your largest garden gnome up as Santa and drape lots of illuminations over everything. Then stand back and watch as the spectacularly unsafe lights catch fire and burn it to the ground in minutes.

Topiary

Bring out the inner artist and turn any large bushes into peacocks and random marsupials. If, after hours of careful clipping and shaping, you are left with a vague blob that looks like a badly savaged shrub instead of a leaping ferret, give in to the rising anger and take a sharp axe to your unhelpful creation. Then get yourself to Great Dixter, a Tudor house in Northiam, East Sussex, where you can weep at how well they have done it while pretending to enjoy the fabulous gardens. If anyone asks about your red eyes say it's hayfever.

Ornamental ponds

As well as providing a haven for newts, toads and cigarette butts, a nice little pond is perfect for unsuspecting animals to drown in, or as a nursery for thousands of mosquitoes, which will rise up in clouds and drain everyone of their thin and precious blood. Putting in a water feature such as a small fountain seems like a great idea until you realise it is actually like Japanese water torture after about five minutes. Before embarking on such a project, closely study the Diana, Princess of Wales Memorial Fountain in Hyde Park, London, a valuable lesson in how to redefine 'incompetent'. Lovely taxpayers' money gushed past like the water its first visitors fell over in. The site had to close for a rethink after only a month and is now patrolled by a team of wardens who prevent people from paddling, which was the whole idea of it in the first place. Good work.

Allotments

Maintaining an allotment is a great alternative if you do not have your own garden. If you are a man, it's a good place to build a small shed and smoke a cheroot, among other manly pursuits. If you are a woman, it's a good place to send your man so you get some peace and quiet around the house. Interestingly, allotments date back over 200 years to the time of the enclosures in the eighteenth and nineteenth centuries. The nice, wealthy landowner objected to some peasants letting their goats nibble a patch of succulent common heath so legislation was passed to allow the commoner access to land for their own use. You might want to think about this as you attack the slugs with pellets, shouting, 'Die, you slimy beasts!'

Allotments really took off in the nineteenth century when Victorians in cities were encouraged to steer their activities away from getting pissed and falling in the gutter. Bear this in mind as you gather a few friends together to drink ginger wine and end up face down in the cabbages. Allotments are now a clever way of growing your own and knowing exactly what goes into them – about half a hernia, some fag ash and quite a bit of alcohol-based pee, mainly. They are now coming back into vogue and, helped on by the organic movement, messing about with spuds has become fashionable once more. So it's practically impossible to get one – an allotment, not a spud.

If you get fed up waiting for the council to assign an allotment to you and you don't have the heart to slip arsenic into old George's pint so you can steal his, the other option is a window box, which can be wonderful for growing herbs such as sage, rosemary and marijuana (strictly for medicinal purposes, you can claim afterwards in court), as well as pretty flowers to attract bees and other dangerous insects into your home.

Chapter Ten

Old Sport

If shearing and pruning in the garden is not enough excitement for you, burn some calories playing sport. It's less hassle than sex and there is a better chance of victory at the end of it. Even though you are gently heading down the other side of the hill, you have the advantages of experience and pity on your side, so seize the initiative and limber up. You might even collect some trophies, which you can sell when money is tight.

Bowls

The popular sport of lawn bowls does not involve locking horns in mortal combat, imminent danger or non-stop action. However, there must be something in it. History buffs believe the Egyptians started bowls off, so you are in good company – unless you get stuck with someone moaning about their knees or how much their sciatica is playing up, in which case shove them into the hedge when nobody is looking.

According to records, the oldest bowling green in use is in Southampton, England, where people have been at it since the year 1299 – and some of the players today look like the original ones. Enjoyed by tubby kings like Henry VIII and favoured by the elderly because you can be as unhealthy as a packet of pork scratchings but still become a champion, it's a kind of relaxation therapy with lots of grass – similar to the 1960s, but a different type of grass.

It's also civilized because when the weather turns cold in autumn, many people play bowls in dryness and comfort indoors until spring. Another perk is that the wearing of white cardigans is actively encouraged. Wear yours with pride as you saunter around the green. The other really lovely thing is that good sportsmanship and being polite and friendly still prevail, and throwing down your bowls and swearing at the umpire will not win you friends or matches. If you are male, do not be put off by the ladies flashing a bit of calf as they bowl in those racy pleated skirts. The saucy minxes are just trying to distract you.

Some useful bowling terms

Burnt end

Rather than a result of the spicy Thai soup you foolishly did battle with last night (that's bowels, not bowls), a burnt end is when the jack gets pushed outside the boundaries of the rink by a bowl that is in play. Normal form is to replay it.

Jack high

Nothing to do with that night down at the pub when Jack took two of those pink pills for his shakes instead of one and sang a faultless version of 'Wind Beneath My Wings'. If a bowl is jack high it signifies that it has reached a position where its nearest part is laterally aligned with the jack. Effectively, it means that the bowl and jack are level.

Toucher

This isn't connected with being a dodgy old perv on the underground at rush hour – a toucher is a bowl that touches the jack before coming to a stop but finishes within the boundaries of the rink. It is usually marked with chalk as it counts towards your score. Interestingly, a toucher remains live even if it ends up in the ditch.

Old spokes' home

In 1818, German Baron Karl von Drais, being an impatient fellow who quickly tired of negotiating the topiary, wanted to get around the royal gardens more rapidly. So he invented a wooden frame with wheels called a hobby horse. Little did he know that he had paved the way for boneshakers, penny-farthings and the modern bicycle. Cycling is a really great way of combating heart disease, diabetes, obesity and other exciting side effects of sitting on your bum all day wondering where the time goes. It's also gentle on your hips, knees and joints.

Running might be great for fun and fitness but it can wear out your knees more quickly than sex on wooden floorboards. With cycling you can go as gently as you like to begin with and gradually build up your fitness.

Cycling glossary

Box of spanners – this is when you are tired out after pushing yourself physically and your riding style gets a bit ugly. It's a poor sign if this happens while just going to the shops for bread.

Break wind – this is cycling so that another cyclist can follow in your slipstream. If you were thinking of something else, get your mind out of the gutter.

Granny gear – the lowest gear available. We find this derogatory in the extreme and will be writing to the relevant organisations to get this phrase changed to 'Age-challenged chain setting'.

SAG station – not connected with the worrying elasticity of your skin. It is a place providing medical or mechanical support on a long recreational ride where lots of people are taking part.

Tandem – the only people in society who can get away with riding the two-person bicycle are old (or tossers). Triumph in being the former and blaze off into the sunset, while muttering about the person behind not pulling their weight.

Tennis

Tennis, like bowls, is a wonderful way of enjoying a sporting battle, and more than a whiff of history pervades it. The game is several thousand years old and was invented by European monks who wanted to have a bit of a laugh in between all those stodgy religious ceremonies with the incense and the wailing. The French royal family got pretty much addicted to real tennis, so named because 'real' means 'royal' in French, and their cries of '*tenez*', meaning 'play', gave birth to the word tennis. The British got the modern game going towards the end of the nineteenth century and in 1881 the first National Men's Singles Championship took place in Newport, Rhode Island. The Americans have been pretty much rabid about the sport of kings ever since.

Chances are you might not beat the record for the oldest person to win a grand slam (Martina Navratilova at 46), but you can certainly die trying. Or you could try to emulate the American, Sheila Johnson of Arizona, who at 60 is the oldest collegiate player in the US but still kicks butt on a weekly basis. The bottom line is plenty of people play into their eighties. The ITF (International Tennis Federation) has a Super Seniors tournament, where the men have an 85 plus category, and the ladies 80 plus. Tournaments are played around the world; have a look at www.itftennis.com when you are in the mood. In May there is also the Cyprus Seniors Tennis Cup, held in Larnaca. They have a 60 plus category so fly down with your racquets and thrash about until you win something, or are ejected.

Superstitious types, tennis players

• Although she relaxed a bit in recent years before retiring in May 2008, Justine Henin-Hardenne never liked to step on any of the lines between points. John McEnroe and many other players also avoid doing this.

• Whenever Andre Agassi served, he always ensured that the ball boys or girls were back in their original positions, going so far as to ask them to switch positions before he would continue.

- Serena Williams likes to wear the same socks throughout an entire tournament. Presumably she washes them.

- The colour yellow is meant to be unlucky and is given a wide berth by players.

- It's meant to be unlucky to hold more than two balls at once, but this might be due to the fact that you will drop them and look inept.

Sailing

Not to be confused with cruising (see Chapter Eleven, or visit your local park). If you have the cash, go and get yourself a lovely little sailing boat – or even a big one. Just don't get an ugly, fume-belching gin palace. Sailing is very much a pursuit of the genteel and grey, especially when they are retired and can stop spending all their money on their children and a bit more on a yacht. Get a salty sea dog cap to complete the image and learn these old phrases to bellow on the water, confirming your maritime knowledge and unsteady temperament:

'I am in the doldrums'

The doldrums refers to the area near the equator where there is frequently little or no wind. This has an excellent double usage as you can be complaining about your life situation while using real sailing terminology to describe being stuck and not really going anywhere. However, getting people to associate you with a lack of wind might take some doing. Another good moment to cry out this phrase in angst-ridden tones is when a large motor-cruiser goes past and unsteadies your boat with its wake, forcing you to fall head first downstairs into the galley while liberally showering yourself with a carefully mixed gin and tonic.

'I feel like I am about to keel over'

Keeling over is when a boat turns over, showing the world its bottom. If you announce this, especially when helming, you will be relieved from your post and told to go and sit on a cushion in the sun and recover, thus excusing you from further duties except using your binoculars to spot attractive people on the beach. Showing the world your own bottom is not the same thing and will lead to mutiny.

'I feel stranded'

Strand was an old word for a beach, so back in the days when men had gold teeth and shoved a cutlass in someone's eye for looking at their cards, if you stuffed up the navigation and ended up on the beach, you were 'stranded'. You were also in deep trouble with the crew but that was a side issue. You can use this expression nowadays to alert your shipmates to the fact that, because you can't read a sea chart, you are about to hit an enormous mudbank. It can also refer to that awful moment when you emerge from a charity shop to find that your electric scooter is up on four bricks with the wheels missing.

Cocktails to keep you seaworthy

Put the 'port' in 'sport' with these invigorating drinks to have at sea. The measurements are in parts as it is the proportions that are important. Use a shot glass or a small jug depending on your tolerance.

Stormy weather

> Ingredients:
> ½ part crème de menthe
> 1½ parts Fernet-Branca
> 1½ parts dry vermouth

Method – pour the ingredients into a small highball glass with ice in it, stir it up a little and serve to captain and crew.

Bahama mama

Ingredients:

1 part dark rum

½ part 151 proof rum (very strong and quite flammable)

½ part coffee liqueur

1 part coconut liqueur

Pineapple juice to fill glass

Juice of half a lemon

Method – mix the ingredients together and pour over broken ice in a Collins glass (taller than a highball). Garnish with a strawberry, sit back and watch the world sail by.

Fuzzy navel

Ingredients:

2 parts lemonade

2 parts peach schnapps

Orange juice to fill glass

Method – pour all of the ingredients into a highball glass, top it off with ice and serve, keeping one eye out for marauding pirates who will stop at nothing to steal your valuable drinks.

Important: you should never be drunk in charge of your boat. Make sure it is someone else's.

Golf

Golf is an unusual sport. Unlike tennis, football or tiddlywinks, it prefers to take up large tracts of pleasant countryside, although if the land wasn't being used as a golf course it would probably be a housing estate. The game's origins are unclear, with the possibility that the word 'golf' comes from the German for a club, *kolbe*, which sounds nothing like it.

What is known is that the Scots were big fans and the first recorded game was played in Edinburgh in 1456. At one time golf was so popular in Scotland that it was banned because it was interfering with archery practice, which was important for national defence. Plus, nobody in senior management was ever at their desk.

Several countries have slightly similar sports, like the ancient game of *chole*, when participants would hit a ball with the minimum number of strokes to reach a target. It is still played in France and Belgium. But it was the Scottish game that developed into the version we know today, and the Royal and Ancient Golf Club of St Andrews is considered the home of the sport.

The modern game is played worldwide and tournaments attract thousands of spectators and big money prizes. There are considerable environmental concerns about the sport, however, and nasty chemicals are sometimes used to produce vivid greens. Golf courses also impede the natural migratory paths of animals – and sometimes humans wanting to take a relaxing stroll without being hit by a little white ball.

Guide to behaving badly on the golf course

1. Act imperiously, swanning about like you own the place. The less you should be behaving like this, the more you will want to. Give in to your insecurities and be rude to as many staff as possible. You are paying good money for the privilege.

2. Be really, really dull, puntuating your conversation with humourless stories about your mediocre existence. It's a popular trait among corporate bores.

3. Wear dreadful clothing such as custard-yellow or sky-blue jumpers and trousers that would look bad on a chef. The sartorial dangers are as numerous as those physical dangers at the seventeenth hole at the TPC in Sawgrass, Florida, which is located on an island.

4. Take an age to play your shot at each hole. If someone tries to hurry you, start barking at them while twitching and turning a deep shade of purple. They will be afraid you are about to drop dead, which would really inconvenience their game, and they will leave you well alone.

5. Push in at the tee. By now the decent golfers out there realise you are a nightmare in human form and will expect nothing less.

Little golfing pleasures for old-timers

Motorised buggies

This is a glorious invention for those who like their golf with minimum effort. As seen in the chapter on pimping your ride, you can easily modify your cart with bumper stickers and 'go faster' stripes. You can even get road legal ones that can cover up to 33 miles after charging overnight – if you are feeling jaded, do not be tempted to plug yourself in.

Off your trolley

Forget humping your clubs over hill and beyond bunker; get a motorised trolley. Not only will you save yourself from physical injury, but you can try to ride it around the greens if you can't afford a buggy. Just don't go off-road into the rough – you will never be seen again.

Hire a caddie

Get some paid support to carry your clubs and dispense advice on how to beat your opponents. While you are responsible for their behaviour on the course, they are free to hide in a bunker or run away into the woods rather than be seen within 50 miles of your tantrums.

Fishing

There is nothing more relaxing than dangling your worm in the water while not thinking of anything – except maybe fishing. Ever since human beings realised that those slimy things in rivers or the sea could end up as pan-fried trout with morels and peas served with unoaked Sauvignon blanc, man has been spearing, netting, hooking and dynamiting fish. Mentioned in the Bible and popular from Persia to China, since marriage was invented husbands have been busy getting away from the wife with a quiet spot of angling. Even the word 'angling' is thought to have come from the man being very nice to the woman for a few days so she is more receptive to the idea of him popping down to the river for a lazy afternoon. With modern inventions like electronic bite alarms, you can even bed down in a small tent and sleep over. This can be a useful alternative to the sofa after a blazing row.

Five fish you don't want to catch:

1. The great white shark – if you hook one of these down at the local pond, you are buggered. Growing to around 24 feet and weighing over 3 tons, it will yank you into the water and blend you into a pink cloud in seconds. At the very least it will get your equipment in an awful tangle.

2. The grizzly bear – it's not a fish, but work with me. You are enjoying a peaceful day's salmon fishing in Canada, possibly in British Columbia. Just as you are reeling a large sockeye in, through the bushes emerges *Ursus arctos horribilis*, looking very horrible indeed. The one thing not to do is run or offer the grizzly your sandwiches if you used low-fat mayonnaise. Do remember that grizzlies run faster than racehorses over short ground. You run slower than a sloth that's been nailed to the ground.

3. The box jellyfish – if you plan to go fishing in Australia, try not to catch one of these highly venomous and squidgy beasts. And don't put it on your head and pretend it's a humorous Halloween mask to your fishing buddies. It will get offended, and you won't like it when it's offended.

4. The blue marlin – one of these bad boys will really pull you off your stool and spill the tea. Weighing in at anything up to 1,000 lb, it will wrench your arms out of their sockets and make you miss your bedtime. Although usually found in warmer waters off the coast of the US, do not be fooled by the serene appearance of that peaceful canal – they are everywhere.

5. The shopping trolley – these are more common in UK waters. Full-grown trolleys have been known to fight for hours before they can be reeled in, testing the stamina and skill of the fisherman to the extreme. But the most dangerous time comes when the fisherman takes his prize home and, on the way, gets his fishing friends to push him around in a supermarket car park at high speed until he falls out of the trolley while cornering.

Watching cricket

We admit it – watching cricket is not a sport, but as you get a bit longer or fewer in the tooth or teeth, the joy of activity is replaced by the joy of watching someone else doing it. Plus, you can drink beer in the process. Those cricketers on the pitch might drive a sleek Mercedes and own several properties, but while they knock a leather ball about under a hot sun, you are the one with an ale in your hand and feet beyond the horizontal.

A game famously described as 'baseball on Valium' sounds rather pleasant, too. The origins of cricket are as hazy as what you did last Thursday. Some say it dates from the thirteenth century, but it can be accurately traced to the sixteenth century. The shepherds of south-east England started playing it when the sheep just weren't doing it for them anymore, using a *cricc*, the Anglo-Saxon word for a shepherd's staff, as a rudimentary bat. It is thought this is where the word 'cricket' came from but even this is disputed. Bloody historians – they wouldn't be able to agree on what colour underpants they were wearing.

It's also a good excuse to wheel yourself out of the house and mingle with polite society. If you are in the stands at a cricket ground, The Barmy Army are an exuberant English mob and actually quite friendly. If you are reasonably elderly and end up sitting near this crowd, they might hoist you aloft as some sort of wartime mascot and fill you full of ale. If you are wealthy, being a member of Lords is ideal for a bit of civilized absorption of cricket while reclining on a comfy white bench in the shade on a summer's afternoon. In the pavilion's Long Room inside, men in jackets and ties behave as gentlemen while cricket's greats look down from paintings and photos. Curtly Ambrose of the West Indies might have once been heckled by some old duffer for a bit of bodyline bowling at Middlesex back in the 1990s, but by and large it remains a cordial affair.

Cricket also gave rise to some memorable lines, one of them belonging to the late commentator Brian Johnston, or Johnners, who was a legend in his own right.

When Neil Harvey was batting for Australia at the Headingley Test in 1961 he famously said, 'There's Neil Harvey standing at leg slip with his legs wide apart, waiting for a tickle.'

Useful phrases:

Stumped – when the wicket keeper has knocked your bails off. Or, you don't know what on earth is going on.

Obstructing the field – when a batsman gets in the way of a fielder trying to field the ball, and a general opinion that many people unfairly have about the elderly.

The Ashes – the trophy for which England and Australia do battle every two years. Nothing to do with you in an urn just yet – that's Chapter Sixteen.

Ball tampering – this is fooling around with the balls, from picking at the seam to using substances apart from saliva in the hope of gaining some sort of advantage – or messing about with that round thing in cricket.

Corridor of uncertainty – the region around the batsman's off-stump, where he will be uncertain whether to try and hit the ball or not – or the aged trying to find the lavatory.

Chapter Eleven

Travel

You may have lots more boxes to tick on the travel insurance forms nowadays, and there is a sneaking feeling that when you conk out halfway up Kilimanjaro the swines are going to leave you there for the hyenas. But plough on regardless – travel is food for the soul; it just needs to be mashed up by someone nice in a uniform now. And there are certain fringe benefits to jetting off to a Hotel Incontinental [sic] for a week. It's hard to describe the joy of ordering a trolley with flashing lights or a wheelchair to whisk you through the airport while the more fleet of foot trudge on carrying their bags. Once past 60, you will also be entitled to all sorts of discounts to things, including entry to National Trust properties or joining ballroom dancing classes.

Even the very nature of holiday photos has changed. Now you build a website or blog with acres of pictures of you standing next to a bus near the Sydney Opera House or the Taj Mahal. So instead of inviting your friends round to bore them senseless with hours of this nonsense, they can be anaesthetised in front of their computer in the comfort of their own home. That's progress.

The bus

The bus is a bastion for the old-timer, not least because they give you a bus pass at 60 so you can ride the thing all day, every day for free. Things have come a long way since the French invented the horse-drawn omnibus in the seventeenth century. Omnibus is Latin for 'for all', but during the daytime this frequently means the greys. Hats must be taken off to 61-year-old Richard Elloway of Wellington, England, who in 2008 became a new kind of intrepid explorer when he travelled from Land's End in Cornwall to John O'Groats in Scotland on his bus pass following the nationalisation of the bus routes. Although, he did have to get special permission for the Scottish leg as the bus pass officially only covers England. It took him a week and nearly 40 buses, and involved getting stranded in Lincoln, reading a lot of bus timetables and quite possibly having a numb bum. He did it to raise money for a children's charity, and you can only hope that they were grateful.

There are a couple of pitfalls to bus travel, however. One is that you become a legitimate target for really ancient, lonely types to come and park their tartan shopping trolley next to you and start telling you about recent complications with their piles. The other is where to sit. Inadvertently end up at the back at the wrong time of day and suddenly 300 schoolchildren will pile on, swearing, screaming and behaving like miniature demons. Nothing will make you hate humanity, and more specifically the junior kind, than being surrounded by a chattering sea of these half-formed monsters with their foul language, as they busily compare mobile phone ringtones. But sit too close to the driver and you will be collared by the old dears and their medical complaints. The ideal position is the 'early middle' of the bus. Several trips to the supermarket and you will be proficient enough in the art of strategic seating to tackle longer journeys.

The coach trip

Like the bus, but hijacked specially by the elderly, often for day trips to places that sell postcards and cream teas. The driver is usually 'a very nice man', and there is sometimes singing, although this tends to fizz people up a bit too much, causing everybody to totally lose control and let themselves down. These trips are not to be confused with National Express coaches, where delights can include drunken football fans fighting at the back and the coach pulling into every insignificant dot of civilization on long journeys.

Top trips for the young at heart and scaly of foot

Bognor Regis

Bognor did wonders for George V in 1929 and, braced with sea air, he gave them the word 'Regis', partly because he was feeling wild and partly because he could, instantly giving restaurant proprietors free rein with the price of scampi. It has long been associated with the elderly, from a gentle spot of shrimping in the nineteenth century to the infirm nodding at one another over a bowl of cream of tomato soup today.

The English Riviera

That's Torquay, Paignton and Brixham for those of you who were asleep in Geography class.

It's like the French one but colder and stuffed with jolly pensioners instead of hot, tanned babes. There are bowling greens, seafronts to promenade on, flower beds in novelty shapes and masses of identical hotels where the carpet looks like someone regurgitated all the bad things they ever ate and the fire escape is possibly unusable. But two nice girls will come in and do a rendition of 'You are my Sunshine' on an electric piano, which is always funny if it happens to be pouring with rain.

Narrowboats

There are more ways that you can get tangled up in a lock on a canal and cause life-threatening foul-ups than you can shake an emergency flare at. But gliding serenely through the backwaters, staring at clouds and wondering what's for dinner is hard to beat.

Birdwatching

'Twitching' can be a good excuse for a night or week away, from spying on bitterns in Norfolk to tracking down shoebills in Uganda. When you were young, you might have owned a catapult, later an airgun or even a shotgun, and birds were there mainly to be knocked out of the sky as a test of eyesight and steady aim. Somewhere around your fortieth birthday, it dawns on you that your aim is lousy, your sight is fading and birds are rather nice to watch instead. It is a link between how close you are to exiting this world and how interesting all the little miracles of nature within it suddenly become. It's also in keeping with the faint notion that one day, not so many years away possibly, you might be standing at the Pearly Gates wishing you hadn't blasted quite so many pigeons to oblivion. It is also loosely connected with wondering about the 'afterlife', and the vague dread that you might come back as a donkey in rural Greece.

Essential kit for the twitcher:

1. Binoculars
2. Bird-spotter's guide
3. Camouflage jacket or olive green attire
4. Hearing aid
5. Sandwiches and flask, map and back door key – after all, you probably haven't left the garden yet

Classic mistakes for the uninitiated

Birdcalls can be confusing. When you start out, often in the garden, your fluffy new companions all seem to make the same kind of noise, demanding expensive nuts and seeds on which to gorge themselves. Begin by trying to identify common birds like the robin and the blackbird. The chiffchaff is also a good one to start with as it is quite easy to identify – it sort of tweets repetitively.

Wading birds rootle about in the mud for their food. Don't wade out too far into the mud to observe them or you will become stuck and have to be craned out by a lifeboat crew who will sell your pictures to the local newspaper. They are mostly unpaid volunteers and need the money.

Know your chiffchaff from your willow warbler. The genuine chiffchaff will be a drabber colour, have shorter wings, a stubbier bill and will warble. Normally, the easiest way to separate these two is by the black legs of a chiffchaff, although this is not always reliable and so is actually not helpful at all.

If while birdwatching close to the sea you pull into a coastal resort or town for lunch or because you are fed up with seeing nothing but ducks, remember that seagulls love chips. While near fast food outlets, keep an eye out for enormous gulls casting a menacing eye over everyone's provisions. Pensioners have been pulled off benches, and it is highly entertaining when it isn't happening to you.

The world's a playground

The University of Lapland in Finland did some studying and found that fooling about in a playground improved a pensioner's balance, dexterity and speed. Then they tried it on a few more pensioners as the first one was bored on his own and was saying 'Can I get off now?' The inner city suburb of Blackley in Manchester has taken the bold step of building a playground for the aged, which is well worth a visit if you are in the area. With a sign reading 'Never too old to play', it is aimed solely at the over-sixties who want to use the six machines, including a ski-walker and a see-saw, and it's excellent for mental and physical well-being as well as a good chinwag. If you enjoy this one, there are similar versions in Germany and Finland. Note that playing kiss chase was banned after someone banged their knee.

Don't be Sarky

Herm, the smallest of the Channel Islands, is perfect for birdwatching, looking at pretty flowers and a secretive snog among the rocks. Being only a mile and a half long, it is ideal for short, manageable strolls and the beach has idle pleasures like picking up lots of different kinds of seashells, which isn't going to overexcite anyone. Sark, part of the Bailiwick of Guernsey, is a favourite because, like Herm, there aren't any cars, meaning you can't hire one and endanger the islanders with your outdated notions about driving. La Coupée, the narrow isthmus connecting the two islands, Greater Sark and Little Sark, only had its railings installed in 1900, and people can remember having to crawl along this connecting strip of land as children where they could have been blown over and lost to the pounding sea. Not so much nature in the raw as stark naked and a bit mental.

I have got problems with my bowls

Not to be confused with complaining about your bowels on holiday, which is a peculiarly British obsession bordering on sport. Imagine the events – the Tapas Triathlon, the Dodgy Curry Derby and Hurling. No, some folk like to travel for a few games of bowls. As well as favourites like Skegness and the English Riviera, short-haul destinations include the ever-popular Spain, where the promise of a 'welcome cocktail' and a 'gala dinner' gets punters twittering like sparrows in the bougainvillea. For the intrepid, you can jet off to Brazil or Argentina, where your game will improve no end if you mix it with a spot of samba.

Cruises

OK, so the *Titanic* didn't go strictly according to plan, but it was memorable. Things have improved since the old days, when a limited number of lifeboats meant there was an undignified scramble to get a place. The only major danger now is getting stuck with that really dull couple from Widnes for the entire trip or catching a dose of virulent food poisoning, which seems to sweep through cruise ships more often than the cleaners. The Mediterranean and the Caribbean continue to be favourites for reclining on a sunlounger and reading a trashy novel until it's time to stimulate yourself with a stiff mojito and a sunset.

Let it all hang out

Have you ever been to a nudist beach? It certainly seems that the saggier your skin, the happier you are in it. This means there is a lot of naked trampolining and frivolity going on among the over-sixties, from France to Florida. Getting lots of naked people round the pool is big business and there are plenty of tour operators to choose from. Just mind your equipment when weightlifting in the hotel gym. If you were hoping for a bit of bareback riding, you might be made to settle for 'textile' horse riding, which is when you have to wear clothes or the horses will run away.

Duffer puffer

With smoking now as popular as anthrax in restaurants and pubs, the canny puffer might want to take his or her dirty habit abroad. The once liberal French have said '*mais non*', as have the Italians, the Swedish and large swathes of Germany – although if large swathes of Germany said '*mais non*' it would be linguistically unusual and incredibly loud. Jump on the Eurostar and go to Belgium, where it is still allowed. They even have special smoking clubs, like the Tabaco in Hasselt, which likes to have a puff and encourages ladies' events with cigars – they have been trying to get Monica Lewinsky over there for years. The Spanish do it as some kind of national pastime and the Austrians have kicked up a huge stink over banning smoking so expect a warm welcome in these places, too.

Singles holidays

There can be rich pickings for those looking for a potential mate, with the benefit of a room of one's own if you get lucky. Often there will be a cultural bent to the trip, but once you find yourself in Venice and the lights go down for the latest production of Cherubini's *Médée*, look around and see how many of your fellow culture vultures are actually just wanting to have a doze in the enveloping dark or leg it to the bar.

Cultural travel

If you like your escapes to involve learning something, possibly using slide shows, laser pointers and academic types who wear bow ties and smell of yeast, the world is your crustacean. Enlightening options range from cooing at the mosques and minarets of Esfahan in Iran to hauling yourself up at dawn to go and see Borobodur. This extraordinary Buddhist monument in Java was rediscovered by Sir Thomas Raffles in 1814, when he stubbed his toe on an unusually solid piece of jungle and shouted something utterly unprintable.

Religious breaks

If you are on a budget, visiting the churches of your native country is free apart from the donation box and you get to accrue some much-needed God points which may save your soul at a later date. Further afield, a pilgrimage to Jerusalem is once-in-a-lifetime stuff unless you go twice, and getting blessed in the Ganges in Varanasi, India, will recharge your karma (just don't swallow the water). If you happen to snuff it here (I *did* say don't swallow the water) it's regarded as the best place in India to do so and the crematorium is open 24/7, which is darkly convenient.

A manageable number of places to see before you die

While the well-known book *1000 Places to See Before You Die* is inspirational and helps promote travel and the experience and wisdom journeys can bring, for the very aged it might be wise to edit it down to a nice, succinct top ten. Maybe even a top three if they involve pulling on shaggy socks and hiking boots and trekking somewhere so remote even McDonald's baulked at setting up a drive-thru there. Or you could just choose options that are within a 5-mile radius of home, have a gift shop with funny fridge magnets and a brace of well-maintained loos.

Did you know...

October 1 is International Day of Older Persons. Organised by the World Health Organisation, they believe that there are 600 million people aged 60 or over worldwide, set to hit two billion in 2050 – that is a lot of slip-on shoes. Events vary from petitions and reports being delivered to governments, to more games of dominoes than usual.

Make it permanent – emigrate

The 'b' in B-plan stands for 'Bugger off abroad and never have to face a cold winter again'. It also neatly excludes you from babysitting duties. Favourite options for the easily pleased include southern Spain, where golf, bowling and slowly drinking yourself into oblivion are well catered for, or Florida, where the local wildlife is a bit more dangerous – they also have alligators. They might still have cold winters in Germany but you could get a warm reception at the Asta Nielsen Haus in Berlin. It's a gay old people's home, where forward-thinking types have decided that once you are a senior citizen, you shouldn't have to explain yourself to anyone. Cyprus is attractive because it is something of a tax haven and has those three lovely words, 'low crime rate', something Croydon does not have.

A word of caution

The bad behaviour of some aged travellers has raised alarm in recent months, forcing the British Foreign Office to do a survey. These so-called 'Saga louts' are often thrill-seekers who mix a carefree skydive with a dash of all-night poolside whisky on the rocks and then wonder why they feel so shipwrecked the next day. Where once it was tattooed twenty-somethings running amok and letting the side down, now it is the turn of the sexagenarian. Just make sure you take out decent travel insurance first.

Useful phrases for old-timers abroad

Hebrew

'Hakadurim hakhadashim hae'le beshvil halev memal'im oti bekhayim.'

'These new heart pills are making me frisky.'

French

'J'ai peut être l'air crevé mais je carbure total.'

'I might look knackered but I still go like a train.'

Spanish

'Estoy aquí por la cirugía estética y el vino barato.'

'I am just here for the cosmetic surgery and cheap wine.'

Russian

'Shto utziba yest shto likhko jzewat?'

'What do you have that is easy to chew?'

Norwegian

'Reisekameraten min har falt overbord i fjorden.'

'My travelling companion has fallen overboard into the fjord.'

Chapter Twelve

Save a Pretty Penny

Face it – life is getting more and more expensive. Successive governments find ever more inventive ways of taxing everyone to bits and pensions are not getting any bigger. But don't start being a miserable git about it. You might lose your hair or keep your teeth in a glass but there is a silver lining. Aside from the odd polite young person who might stand up and give you a seat on the bus, other benefits include stuff you now get for free. So if you have been a foolish thing and failed to stash enough money away, don't panic. Just because they have cut the gas off and debt collectors are readying the removals van, you can save money in unexpected areas.

Wheels and deals

The bus pass

As we've seen earlier, the free bus pass will land on the mat when you turn 60. Cheer yourself at reaching this milestone by cruising at low speeds into town to wander aimlessly, get in people's way and waste shop assistants' time by asking them to demonstrate how things that you have no intention of buying work.

Bungee jumping

Some companies will give you a free jump if you are past a certain age. Secretly, the reason is, after years of doing it, the instructors are bored silly watching healthy people jumping and surviving and they are trying to increase their chances of filming someone croaking mid-dangle.

Skydiving

Likewise, some skydiving centres might give you a free or reduced tandem jump. The medical questionnaire will take a week but the emotional high of the wind shrieking past you as you drop at 120 mph towards the ground can only be matched by the last ever episode of *Dad's Army*.

Supermarket coupons

Not entirely in the same league as jumping out of an aeroplane, but the rush you get when you receive a free jar of beetroot is reasonably special. There are websites dedicated entirely to free things you can send off for, such as: www.free-stuff.co.uk. If you have little money and a lot of time (unlike those still working who have little money and absolutely no time) it is a bit more constructive than just watching the Windows screensaver and hoping it will do something interesting soon.

Libraries

They're warm, smell faintly of books and run by people who frequently don't know where anything is. But once you have left the house, consider popping into your local library to find out the melting point of zinc and to borrow books, audio books and DVDs at reasonable prices. It is always a good idea to use fake ID which you bought on the Internet because if you are forgetful (and that is a generous 'if') you will run up hundreds of pounds in late fees because you got so cross at how bad the best-selling *The Da Vinci Code* was that you threw it on the fire, before you remembered it wasn't yours, to put it out of its misery.

Rootle

'Wild food' might have become popular thanks to the odd woolly celebrity chef or Ray Mears rootling about in the undergrowth for fungi, but the OAP who has blown the monthly allowance on a comical letter-opener or hand-engraved backscratcher can save a tidy sum with what Mother Nature provides in the giant larder that is the countryside. Get yourself a wicker basket and take a stroll into the woods; not only do you get some exercise but it's all for free. If you really get hooked on combing the land for calories, there is an annual Really Wild Food & Countryside Festival in St David's in Wales every year, where you can go for a group fumble in the hedgerows without getting arrested. See www.reallywildfestival.co.uk for details.

Plants

Edible milk thistles, nettle omelette, dandelion cordial – the list of greenery you can pilfer is vast. Wild garlic is actually believed to be better for you than regular garlic and it jazzes up a summer salad or soup very nicely. Fat hen, a wild plant, has more protein and iron than spinach. Most plants can be steamed or boiled like standard vegetables. In the summer months blackberries are delicious and great in jams or crumbles. Then there are crab apples, elderberries, hawthorns and rosehips. Acorn tagliatelle will impress your friends. Sloes, which can be picked in September and October, are used to make winter-warming sloe gin, which will have you drunk in minutes. And there is absolutely nothing wrong with setting up camp next to an apple tree and brewing your own cider while living rough for a couple of days.

Fungi

Puffballs the size of footballs can feed you for a week. Oyster mushrooms might cost a bomb at a local market but they are probably sprouting for free just up the road. Just make sure you carry a book to identify the different species. You can also do courses and go out with experts country wide to avoid picking poisonous mushrooms and going wheels up after making quiche using the cheerfully named 'destroying angel'.

Animals

Road kill, if still warm, can be good. Pheasants, deer and badgers are all edible, and with practice you will soon be exploring the delights of pigeon tikka masala. Swerving deliberately to hit things or laying down food as bait to entice animals onto the road is not to be encouraged. Neither is accelerating when you see those signs with a deer on them.

Fish

There's nothing like standing in a river with a home-made spear for reconnecting with your inner primitive. However, the fishing licence people might not see it this way. Better still, head out to sea and snaffle a mackerel with a rod and a fly. Some people are worried about rising pollution and the mercury content of fish but we are all going to hell in a hand-basket anyway. Better to embrace oblivion with limited mental capacity than to fully comprehend the ghastliness of it all.

Things you can burn for fuel

When things get really tough in the depths of winter, you can save money by burning stuff.

1. **Your spouse** – when they pop their clogs, this can save a fortune on cremation fees and really cuts down on red tape. It will also keep the house warm for a couple of days, but maybe save those marshmallows for another time – dignity and all that.

2. **The furniture** – old-fashioned sofas and chairs containing highly flammable foam will look spectacular but only throw out intense heat for a short time, as well as setting fire to the chimney and possibly reducing your house to smouldering rubble. Better to find some good, solid wooden pieces, like pine chairs. Burning the kitchen table will mean you don't

have to invite the children round for Sunday lunch ever again – unless they bring trays for TV dinners.

3. Wood foraged from the land – driftwood, branches blown down in gales or the neat pile of logs in your neighbour's backyard are all good options.

4. The net curtains – if you have done a lot of frying over the years they may go up rather suddenly. Watch your eyebrows – they are bushier and hence highly flammable these days.

5. Old clothes

6. Your entire collection of *Steam Railway Magazine*

7. Not your entire collection of *Playboy* from the 1970s – sell it on eBay.

8. All the books in the loft you never read anyway – this will save a huge headache for your offspring when you shuffle off this mortal coil.

9. All those supermarket coupons you are never going to get round to using

10. The doors – this might also help the heat to circulate around the house. Maybe leave the one on the loo.

Chapter Thirteen

Food and Drink

Unless you have a gold card with Meals on Wheels, it's good to know how to boil an egg and generally survive. But as you begin to no longer feel like the sharpest tool in the box, stave off going a bit gaga with a powerful mix of intelligent foodstuffs. And then undo all the good work with some mind-bending traditional cocktails.

Brain food

Coffee

Those boffins in white coats in the US have decided that a cup of coffee a day might help prevent Alzheimer's. Drink too much full-strength Colombian, however, and you will get the shakes anyway.

Liver

Not everyone's favourite, but liver is known to help produce Acetylcholine (ACh), one of the three key neurotransmitters that help to keep the grey matter functioning. Your grandchildren might think liver is foul and so happily give you theirs when their parents aren't looking.

Tomatoes

Lycopene, an antioxidant found in tomatoes, helps prevent dementia. This fruit is actually part of the nightshade family and when the Spanish brought them to Europe from South America, they just grew them for fun and called them 'love apples'.

Wholegrains

Stock up on things like wheat bran and cereals as they help your memory. Wheat bran is full of vitamins, proteins and iron, and is very good at combating the dreaded c-word: constipation.

Oily fish

Generally good for the mind, but with the added boost that iodine is wonderful for a bit of mental clarity. After a few weeks, you might be standing next to the sardines in the supermarket and for once not staring into space thinking, 'Now what did I come here for?'

Blueberries

These are related to huckleberries and bilberries and you can tell genuine blueberries because there are small, granular dots on their twigs. Research shows that they improve short-term memory loss so there are no more excuses for not knowing where you left the car – or the blueberries.

Sage

The name says it all. Use fresh or in oil form to raise your levels of wisdom and finally get at least one question right on *University Challenge*. The herb version is also a lot more enjoyable than the book-keeping software made by a company of the same name. Let's all go wild and do some accounting.

Nuts

Good for energy and can stave off depression and elevate the mood. Also perfect for throwing at your spouse to see if they can catch them in their mouth. Be wary of telling partners about your fondness for Brazilians – they might start pouring hot wax on your nether regions.

Ration yourself

Many old-timers will recall that you didn't see lots of obese children back in post-war Britain. This was partly due to rationing and a fundamental lack of certain foodstuffs, coupled with more healthy exercise and playing in the street. Nowadays, they are sitting with a can of Coke, slumped in front of an Xbox while trying to work out whether ordering pizza or getting some crisps from the kitchen frees up more playing time on *Pointless Carnage 5*. During World War Two, the British government had a wonderful scheme called 'Dig For Victory' to encourage plucky Brits to grow their own vegetables. 'Dig Because I Am Bloody Ravenous' didn't get past the planning phase.

Recreate a post-war dish today

Mock goose

Ingredients:

1.5 lb of potatoes

2 large cooking apples

4 oz of Cheddar cheese

One teaspoon of dried sage

Salt and pepper

¾ pint of vegetable stock

1 tablespoon of flour

Method – slice the potatoes quite finely, then slice the apples and grate the cheese. Have a little rest. Then place a layer of the potatoes in a greased oven dish, cover with the apples and some sage (still feeling wild about accounting), season lightly and sprinkle with the cheese. Do this a few times to build up layers and keep enough potatoes and cheese to top it all off. Pour in half a pint of the stock and cook at a moderate temperature for 40 minutes. Blend the flour with the remainder of the stock, pour into the dish and cook for another 15 minutes. Serve with vegetables like spinach or broccoli. Then realise that this recipe is just to mock you since it is nothing like goose. There was also a mock duck recipe made with red lentils that you moulded into a duck shape, which must have led to a bit of a shock when people ate real duck.

Not exactly fried sausages

Ingredients:
1lb of potatoes
White cabbage
A generous handful of breadcrumbs
Caraway seeds
Salt and pepper

Method – steam the cabbage and potatoes until nice and soft, then blend them up roughly in a food processor or put them through a mincer if you are still living in the Dark Ages. Add the caraway seeds and season with salt and paper, shape the mixture into sausages of whatever size and shape makes you happy, and gently fry for a few minutes until they look like they aren't going to get any better.

Definitely not fudge

Ingredients:

Four medium-sized carrots

Gelatine

Grated rind of an orange

Method – grate the carrots quite finely and cook four full tablespoons in just enough water to cover for ten minutes. Add the grated orange rind to give it some kick. Melt a small amount of gelatine and add to the mixture. Keep stirring while cooking for a few minutes. Spoon into a flat-bottomed dish, allow it to set and then dice it into cubes and serve to your guests while keeping alive the charade that it is remotely like fudge.

A little tipple

You can undo all the virtuous self-denial of the above with these old-fashioned drinks with a touch of class. There are some delicious old-school drinks out there and you never know, your local barman at the pub might be able to make some of them. Failing this, put out the cat and have a cocktail party at home – you will be in the recovery position for days. As seen in the nautical cocktails in Chapter Ten, the recipes below use parts as the measurement and a shot glass would be the most logical container. Use a watering can if you love a challenge.

The Old-fashioned

It's got your name written all over it. It is believed to have been created by a barman at the Pendennis Club in Louisville around 1900. Colonel James E. Pepper, a Kentucky-based bourbon distiller and a customer at the bar, took it to New York, where it became famous. Cole Porter penned a song called 'Make it Another Old-fashioned, Please', and at one time it was known as the 'palate-paralyser', which has a warning in there somewhere.

Ingredients:
2 measures of bourbon
A dash of Angostura bitters
1 sugar cube
Soda water

Method – place a sugar cube in an old-fashioned glass (it's like a big tumbler) and soak with the Angostura bitters. Add enough soda to cover the sugar cube and crush it using a spoon. Add the bourbon and top up with soda. Give it all a stir and finish with a slice of orange and a maraschino cherry. Drop a twist of lemon in the drink and stand well back.

The sidecar

This surfaced in the early part of the twentieth century and is rumoured to have been invented by Harry from Harry's Bar in Paris, where it was created for an army captain who was driven to the bar in a motorcycle sidecar. The name might have also come from the fact that if you had too many, there was no way you were going to be the one riding the motorbike.

Ingredients:
1 part brandy
1 part triple sec
1 part lemon or lime juice

Method – fill a shaker with ice, put everything in together, give it a good shake and strain into a cocktail glass.

The bosom caresser

This might cause a raised eyebrow or a hearty slap if you order it in a bar, but is mildly better than asking for a 'slippery nipple'. It came into being in the 1920s and is attributed to cocktail legend Harry Craddock at the American Bar in the Savoy Hotel.

Ingredients:

2 parts brandy

1 part orange curaçao

A dash of grenadine

1 egg yolk

Method – pour all of the ingredients into a shaker full of ice, give it a good shake and strain into a small wine or cocktail glass.

The corpse reviver

Highly relevant to those who are feeling jaded by the passage of time, this little number was cooked up at the Savoy in 1930 and features in the *Savoy Cocktail Book*. The original consists of a mix of gin, Cointreau, lemon juice, vermouth and absinthe.

Ingredients:

1 part gin

1 part lemon juice

1 part Cointreau

1 part vermouth

A dash of absinthe

Method – splash a little absinthe in a chilled coupe or Martini glass, then combine the other ingredients in a shaker full of ice. Shake and pour into the glass. Then let the growing-old pains just slip away.

Babycham

Remember when this stuff came out? You were probably too drunk at the time. Shepton Mallet's gift to society in 1953, this infamous pear cider cleverly targeted women who were fed up with cream sherry through television adverts which featured a small, excitable cartoon deer. It was an instant smash, predominantly in terms of drunken accidents.

Chapter Fourteen

Pets Cornered

To stave off loneliness and jolly things along around the house, those of mature years often resort to keeping an animal. Not only does it give you something to fuss over and talk about, but studies have shown that pets have a positive effect on mood and well-being as well as keeping you physically active. They also offer companionship and loyalty, give your day some routine and they don't disappear down the pub for hours or spend the housekeeping budget on double vodkas.

Pets that aren't a total nuisance

Dogs

The shih-tzu is a switched-on, amiable little fellow who will love to be matey with you. However, clip its coat regularly to make it more manageable or face losing hours of valuable daytime TV grooming the damn thing. Bear in mind that a full clip-job is a bit harsh in the middle of winter so pick your season carefully. The Pomeranian resembles a small teddy bear and is endearing. They can be lively but this means that they can also be noisy and hence a complete pain. Although pugs have a face like they have been bashed in with a shovel, they are friendly, intelligent little beasts who are easy to manage. Their snoring can give the man of the house a run for his money.

Adult greyhounds, contrary to popular opinion, can actually be lazy swines, happy to snooze for hours at a stretch. A good-natured breed, do not count on them to make you a bit of cash down at the track. Don't forget how useful the dog can be for fetching slippers – and dog-walking is a great euphemism for nipping to the pub.

Avoid puppies, however; there's nothing worse for the knees and back than constantly having to bend down to clear up the wee (and worse) that your lovely new puppy has thoughtfully left inside your slippers.

Cats

They're moody, self-indulgent and they use the flowerbed as a toilet. But when you have stopped berating your grandchildren, have a think about a cat as a pet. In medieval times they were associated with witchcraft and treated rather badly. Unlike a dog, a cat will not recycle the newspaper before you have read it, and will quickly fit in with your routine of not doing very much all day long. Cats can also be useful for keeping your lap warm, but won't be much use if confronted by a burglar – they will simply flirt outrageously and ask to be fed.

Birds

Budgerigars are an obvious choice for those with limited energies. Colourful and low-maintenance, they can be left to wander the carpet, trained to fetch you snacks and reply to emails. They can also live for 15 years so they might outlive you. Parrots, on the other hand, are beady little fellows who are happier to be handled but are also a handful. They can go mad if you don't give them enough attention so train yours to shriek obscenities and make sure they know exactly which family members to attack. This can be achieved by showing them colour photographs of the intended target and rewarding them with treats.

Tortoises

Not one for the thrill-seeking adrenaline addict, but a solid, dependable companion until it wanders off through the hedge and is never seen again. If you can't keep up with your pet tortoise walking round the garden, you really are past it. Like you, they also enjoy calcium supplements and they can live for a hundred years, so do remember to pass them on to someone patient in your will.

Pets that might not be such a great idea

Elephants

Male African elephants can grow to 12 feet tall and weigh around 15,000 lb. This has got 'Pensioner Flattened in Jumbo Horror' written all over it.

Tigers

Tiger cubs might be little cuties to romp around with in the garden, but one day when they are bigger one of them will get carried away and sink its 5-inch claws into your back and it will all go pear-shaped. Even worse than a man with a bad aim in the household, tigers mark their territory like randy fountains. You will also need a lot of land to keep them. If you insist on getting one, keeping it in the shed on your allotment will guarantee nobody fools with your prized cucumbers again.

Poisonous snakes

Non-poisonous ones actually make good, placid pets, but when you walk into the pet shop the owner might spy his only chance to offload that spitting cobra that was meant to be a garter snake. You will only realise something is amiss when it's busy blinding the dog.

Sharks

Even with inventive use of the pond and re-housing the goldfish, keeping a shark might prove difficult. Most full-grown adults will need a space the size of a swimming pool, and it will be forever ruining the lilos. You can cram a reef shark into an aquarium in the house, but first pause to reflect on how you would like being stuffed into a confined space with nothing to do but aimlessly drift backwards and forwards for the rest of your days.

Lobsters

It takes seven years for a lobster to reach a weight of approximately 1 lb. It takes seven seconds to say 'lobster thermidor' really slowly. One day there is bound to be a conflict of interest and horrid scenes involving boiling water.

Animal facts

- Butterflies have around 12,000 eyes. They spend most of their short lives looking for their reading glasses.

- An adult blue whale's heart beats about six times a minute. It slows to four when it hears Terry Wogan.

- The oldest recorded goldfish lived for 41 years. Its dying words were 'Thank God'.

Chapter Fifteen

Let's Get Physical

There's nothing more exciting than having a good conversation about your maladies, and as the years fall by more and more falls off, giving you plenty of subject matter. There are a range of health issues to consider and any one could affect you.

The flu jab

The canny coffin-dodger starts to get excited in the autumn when the leaves fall from the trees and people start to sniff a lot, as colds and flu descend on society like uninvited relatives. This is when a judicious visit to the doctor to have the annual flu jab is called for, ideally sometime between late September and early November. You need to be immunised annually as the strains vary from year to year.

Flu is not to be sneezed at either. In the winter of 1918/1919 the infamous Spanish flu broke out and people couldn't stop feverishly playing castanets and doing the Macarena.

In 1976, when a soldier in New Jersey died of swine fever, normally only seen in pigs, scientists were puzzled. When eight more soldiers were found with the same strain, they wondered if someone had been having a bit too much fun with the animals. Swine fever is not to be confused with the wonderfully named, but probably not that funny, hog cholera.

The flu vaccine was discovered in 1944 and is now a big feature in the old-timer's social calendar. Flu is transported by coughs and sneezes so don't get too close to anyone from September onwards. If you are allergic to hens' eggs, you shouldn't have the jab as it is made from this. The flu jab does not cover avian flu and if you insist on kissing chickens your dirty secret will be your undoing.

DIY anti-wrinkle cream

A wrinkle is a crease on the surface of the skin. It's also a sign of ageing that nobody wants. You could spend a fortune on complicated lotions and potions full of exciting things nobody has ever heard of, or try the following inappropriate alternatives:

Animal fat

Roman women used refined animal fats in their face cream. You might smell like yesterday's bacon but your skin will be baby-smooth.

Emu oil

Made from the refined fats of emus, this has been used by the Aborigines in Australia for thousands of years. It is also meant to be good for reducing the signs of ageing. To keep costs down, you will have to poach some emus from a local farm and process their fat yourself, which could be dangerous and wreak havoc with your shoes.

Mayonnaise

Forget chicken sandwiches – rubbing a bit of mayonnaise into your face at night works a treat. The dog will lick you awake with more enthusiasm than normal.

Haemorrhoids cream

Models have allegedly used piles cream around their eyes to get rid of puffiness. The Norwegian manufacturer concerned actually appealed to people to use it properly, after wasting an entire morning in the boardroom laughing at how dumb models can be.

Medicinal side effects, some of them pleasant

Hallucinations

Some anti-depressants, anti-fungal or Alzheimer's medication can cause all sorts of visual disturbances, from imagining the trees in the garden are growing as you are watching them to seeing snakes writhing across the carpet towards you. Before you get cross that there are polar bears in the living room again, remember that in the 1960s people paid good money for this.

Inability to sit down

Taking a dose of Viagra is all fine and large, but do be aware that, in rare cases, erections can last for more than four hours.

This could well be three hours and 55 minutes too long for a lot of people. Known as priapism, this can actually damage the penis. A small number of people have also experienced a sudden loss of vision, but this can be handy if you are having sex with someone who isn't exactly an oil painting.

Passing out

This is the main goal of millions of teenagers across the world every Friday and Saturday night. You have cleverly bypassed a great deal of liver damage, kebabs and general financial and physical hardship by taking pills that didn't entirely agree with you. Enjoy the disconnected bliss, we say, and then milk your relatives for maximum sympathy and expensive chocolates when you regain consciousness.

Places to talk about your ailments

The post office queue

Strangers of a similar seniority have a built-in radar for recent surgery or troublesome cataracts. Start with a gentle enquiry about someone's health and they will immediately tell you about their swollen ankles. Let them run with it for a minute or two, then exclaim 'That's nothing! Last week my knee was oozing pus the colour of an unripe mango'. Don't forget that if you go heavy on the gore and bodily leakage, you might be able to halve the queue as delicate customers have to leave, especially if you casually drop in the phrase 'highly contagious'.

The supermarket

Lurk in the aisle with the cosmetics and medicines. When another old-timer starts looking at different brands of phlegm-loosener, move in, dispense an opinion on which kind is better and then say, 'You're lucky it's just your lungs. Last week I sneezed and half my brain shot out and landed on the mantelpiece. It scared the parrot to death.'

The workplace

If you still work, your co-workers are a captive audience. Secretly they are actually interested because face it – drafting financial reports is even more dull than your awful ailments.

Old people's homes

If you are not actually a resident, sneak in through the conservatory one lunchtime and strike up a conversation with the inmates over the soup. They will be grateful for the company and will happily discuss any illness, disease or medical procedure until they nod off or the staff discover you.

How to put people off their food

If you are in a crowded restaurant, hospital or at a busy family dinner, there are several ways to put people off their food and double your calorific intake at no extra cost. Favourites include:

- 'I sneezed and burst all the stitches.'

- 'They said they had never seen a tapeworm that long. Actually, it looked a bit like your tagliatelle.'

- 'I always forget to wash my hands after going to the loo. My genital warts medication makes me forgetful. Bread rolls, anyone? They're still warm.'

- 'The first thing I wanted to eat in hospital after they operated on my piles was meatballs. Don't ask me why.'

Dentures

What not to say

If you are new to the joys of false teeth, when you laugh, cough or smile this can cause them to come unstuck. There are also certain words that might be difficult to say at first. Do not show these tongue-twisters to your grandchildren. They will take the Michael out of you for the rest of your life when you explode in a fit of lisps and dribble. Instead, quietly practise them on your own.

1. Six sick slick slim sycamore saplings

2. I slit the sheet, the sheet I slit, and on the slitted sheet I sit

3. We surely shall see the sun shine soon

4. Six shimmering sharks sharply striking shins

5. Mrs Smith's fish sauce shop

What not to eat

1. Toffee

2. Nuts

3. Steak

4. Gravel

5. Anyone older than you

What not to do with a dicky heart

Go to Las Vegas

You know perfectly well you will only blow your winnings on prostitutes and angel dust. Stay at home and listen to jazz.

Put the life savings on the Grand National

Having a flutter on the horses will take on a whole new dimension as you watch your hard-earned cash fall at the first hurdle and your chest starts tingling. Guaranteed for palpitations and levels of terror in proportion to how much you stand to lose, and how far up that remote creek without a toothpick you will be.

View too many episodes of *Columbo* in one sitting

Peter Falk inspired legions of fans around the world as the scruffy detective with a canny knack for solving crimes, and the suspenseful series aired between 1971 and 2003 from Argentina to the Ukraine. The episode called 'Dead Weight', when Lieutenant Columbo's mysterious first name is finally revealed, might prove too exciting for your delicate disposition.

Watch the World Cup

A German study found that cases of heart attacks went up during World Cup matches. Penalty shoot-outs are particularly good at loading you up with blood-clotting stress that will make your arms go numb and your family start to idly wonder how much the house is worth. Take up lawn bowls instead – there is far more drinking and fighting involved but the tension is manageable.

Christmas

'Tis the season to go blue in the face and nosedive into the carpet when the cocktail of bad television, family tantrums and screaming grandchildren all reaches a crescendo at 3 p.m. On the positive side, a quick death saves you from having to write thank you cards for tat you didn't want.

Flatulence

It might be funny for everyone else until you inadvertently gas them in a confined space like a lift or a cupboard, but farting is no laughing matter when it reaches uncontrollable proportions. Some medication for type 2 diabetes has the alarming side effect of excessive flatulence. Bacteria in the colon are able to partly digest fibre that bacteria in the intestines can't, but produce gas in the process. Flatulence-free beans have been developed in the UK using the manteca bean from Chile, but where the fun is in that remains unclear.

You can try anti-flatulence pills or charcoal-lined pads that go in the underwear and defuse any malodorous emissions. But the best cure is those everyday situations when you can safely blow off and not be heard. Do be careful, however, as in most social circumstances everyone blames the old-timer, so the dice are already loaded against you.

Top moments to get away with it

The football match
Liverpool fans are reputed to be the loudest but Real Madrid fans aren't afraid of deafening everyone within earshot. Games in Italy

and Spain tend to be peppered with drums and horns, meaning you can safely blast in unison if you have a good sense of timing.

When trying out your new siren
Buy a Vortex R4 air-raid siren. When you need to make a noise, this monster will put you to shame with an output of 129 decibels. You must realise, however, that you will damage yourself and anyone else nearby, the entire neighbourhood will think a tornado or nuclear missile is about to level the street and the authorities will come running, possibly with unsmiling faces and big guns.

At a gig
If you just happen to be passing by, drop in and see Gallows, the British hardcore punk band. You might stand out like a pair of dog's testicles among the young revellers but they claim to be the loudest band in the world after once notching their noise up to 132.5 decibels. Nobody will notice a trouser cough in amongst this sort of brain-splintering chaos.

While swimming near an excited blue whale
Balaenoptera musculus, or the blue whale to his blubbery friends, lets out a highly structured, repetitive, low-frequency rumbling noise that can travel for many miles underwater, possibly even across oceans – a bit like you in the bath. The sound has been recorded at 188 decibels, which is pretty good considering humans shout at about 70 decibels. The theory is that they are communicating with

other whales and trying to get a bit of sex on the off-chance. An aquatic and speculative 'Your sea or mine, baby?'.

Krakatoa
You have missed the boat with this volcanic Indonesian island, but if you had been in Indonesia and feeling windy in 1883, the already troublesome volcano blew itself to bits in a series of explosions so violent and loud they destroyed most of the island and were heard as far away as Perth in Western Australia, over 1,900 miles away – where someone quickly coughed in case that strange noise was coming from them.

Cosmetic surgery

The British are now spending £1 billion a year on cosmetic surgery, from teeth whitening to full facelifts. Contrary to popular belief, a lot of demand for cosmetic surgery comes from people in their seventies and eighties who want to turn back the clock, rather than hormonally imbalanced teenagers hypnotised by the airbrushed shallowness of modern aesthetics. Women are the market leaders but men are starting to get in on the action and under the knife.

The facelift
When the toll of the years becomes too much, poke Father Time in the eye and run for the scalpel. As the skin sags with

age, so a facelift will make you look younger and half-alive again. At the very least, you won't have people coming up to you and checking your pulse when you fall asleep on the bus. Go for a full facelift, or areas like the brow or the neck.

Botox

This naturally occurring protein is one of the most toxic things in the world. The CIA soaked some of Fidel Castro's cigars in it but never went ahead with assassinating him this way because it just didn't seem right to top someone when they were having a thoughtful cigar, possibly on the loo. Then some genius thought it would be good to inject it into your face for a perkier appearance. This could go wrong one day and recent evidence that it ended up in the brains of laboratory mice might make you nervous – look fabulous, feel thick.

Boobs

Those days of silicone breasts exploding on flights and overturning the drinks trolley are over. Enlarge with confidence.

Netherlands

If the idea of buttock implants puts a smile on your face, just wait until you get a load of vaginal tightening.

It shouldn't happen to a celebrity

Famous people are naturally drawn to cosmetic surgery, often because they have an excess of money and bugger-all common sense. In the artificially enhanced hall of shame we have:

Donatella Versace
She has lips like an exotic species of carp that swam into the side of the pond at great speed.

Kenny Rogers
The American musical legend didn't like his squinty eyes and had them lifted. Now they are too tight and he looks permanently startled. Maybe there was something more to 'Eyes That See in the Dark', after all.

Joan Rivers
Bless her nipped and tucked cottons, but Joan overdid it a bit. For someone who spent a fair amount of time under the scalpel, she can be a bit cutting herself, but on the good side she likes animals and actively campaigns for their rights.

On your toes

You knew there was a reason you were so loving and nice to your partner all these years/days/since last Sunday, and as any wise senior will tell you, it's when you realise you can't bend down to cut your toenails any longer that you will need help from someone who is just as happy filing down your verrucas with an emery board as sucking your toes with gay abandon – simultaneously, if they are talented.

Smoking

You may be from a generation that was told that smoking was good for you, and any host who didn't put out a bowl of cigarettes for their guests was considered mean. As with many health issues, scientists like to swing both ways (eggs, getting a dose of sun, red wine, having a drink during pregnancy), and eventually smoking will be better for you than eating fruit. Brilliant.

Chapter Sixteen

Death - Deal with It

Possibly the most worrying thing about time is that one day you, me and that annoying man who couldn't remember his PIN number in the newsagent this morning will all be dead. Forget Benjamin Franklin, with his views on death and taxes being unavoidable. There are loads of ways of getting round tax, from forming a sect in the desert and heavily arming yourself to swanning about in Switzerland and getting lost in the Alps. But Death levels all with his sharpened sickle and stand-up comedy routine. You should see his impression of Joan Rivers; it'll kill you.

Be different

We all know the usual ways of kicking the bucket, from heart attacks to watching party political broadcasts until your brain leaks out of your nose. But if you want to stand out from the herd, opt for the departure with a difference.

Aeroplane crash

You have to be something of a rarity to peg it in a plane crash. It is nearly as hard as enjoying the food. The tail section or anywhere close to an exit are thought to be the safest places to sit. Go and sit at the front, but not too close to the doors, and distract the pilots if on a small craft with relaxed security. You can lessen your chances of survival when exiting in an emergency by remembering to take your duty-free booze and oversized novelty panda with you. If you crash in a desert, leave the plane and walk off aimlessly into the middle of nowhere, taking as little water as possible.

Shark attack

We all saw *Jaws* and got nervous just standing in a puddle afterwards. Or maybe the puddle was *because* of the nerves. Either way, your chance of dying by becoming a petit four for a savage fish is about one in 300 million. Your chances of going via a car crash are about one in 200 in the UK. The answer is obvious – we need to ditch cars and drive sharks instead.

Lightning

It's funny stuff, lightning – unless you happen to get hit by it. Odds vary but it's around a one in three million chance. Travelling at a knicker-tearingly rapid 14,000 mph, a bolt carries around 300,000 volts to the earth and heats the air around it to about 30,000 °C, which is roughly half as hot as Seville in July.

If you want to up the ante, move to Uganda, where they have storms most days. If you find yourself climbing a mountain in Africa and see some baboons whose fur is standing on end, making them look like nervous puffballs, it is time to get off the mountain very quickly. People wearing jewellery often get branded by it if they are struck so sporting that heart-shaped pendant with 'Forever yours' written on the back will give you a nice, tasteful tattoo if you survive. If you are sweaty or rain-soaked, the water can turn to steam, sometimes causing your shoes and clothes to be blown off. Golfers are statistically the most at risk, along with fisherman, which is quite handy as

losing their clothes and shoes would make the average golfer less of a weeping sore on the face of fashion.

Wasp sting

Your chances of dying from anaphylactic shock following a wasp sting are about one in 57,000. Boost your odds by moving to the countryside, consuming very sweet drinks in the garden during the summer and swatting half-heartedly at them with a newspaper so that they become bruised and angry. If you have apple trees, put a half-eaten apple from the ground in a jam jar to entice wasps to enter. Shake it so all the wasps are in a seething rage, and then open it in your underwear.

Not winning the lottery and then having a heart attack

You might be lured every week by the oft-repeated mantra that someone has to win it, but there is naff-all chance it is ever going to be you. The chances of winning the UK lottery stand at one in 14 million. The chances of dying of a heart attack are slightly better at one in seven. It takes a lot of complex maths to skilfully blend these two figures together, but suffice to say you have a much better chance of causing yourself to blow a fuse by getting really angry at the television when you fail to scoop the jackpot for yet another week running. Jumping up and down on your torn-up ticket adds to the already murderous atmosphere.

Put some irony in your diet

Across history, fate has confirmed it has a wicked sense of humour.

Aeschylus

In 500 BC a talented Greek playwright called Aeschylus was widely regarded as the father of Greek tragedies and it was only fitting that he should go and suffer one himself. Where he lived, eagles used to scoop up tortoises and drop them on rocks to crack them open. One day an eagle mistook his bald head for a rock and dropped a tortoise right on him, which killed him. The tortoise survived, although it laughed so much it nearly burst a lung.

Attila the Hun

In AD 453 the ferocious Attila married a young girl named Ildico. Normally, the feared leader was quite conservative and didn't overdo it on the food and booze at banquets but he really cut loose on his wedding night and gorged himself. He suffered a massive nosebleed in the night and, being rotund with foodstuffs and utterly hammered, drowned in his own blood.

Alexander Bogdanov

A very clever Russian physician and scientist, Bogdanov was convinced that humans could rejuvenate themselves through blood transfusion. In 1928 he was given the blood of a student who later turned out to be suffering from tuberculosis and malaria. Bogdanov died.

Jerome Irving Rodale

The architect of the organic food movement in the US. In the thirties he set up Rodale Press, an important publishing business, which produced *Organic Farming and Gardening* magazine in 1942. While on *The Dick Cavett Show*, a US talk show, the 72-year-old Rodale had just announced 'I'm going to live to be a hundred unless I'm run down by a sugar-crazed taxi driver' and 'I never felt better in my life', when he died of a heart attack. The show was never aired on television, and the rather lively taxi drivers queuing up outside to flatten him were discreetly shooed away.

Jim Fixx

Author of the best-selling *Complete Book of Running*, which had everyone putting on bad headbands and taking up jogging in the seventies, Fixx went for a jog while visiting Vermont. He then died of a massive heart attack. His autopsy revealed that his coronary arteries were all seriously blocked. However, he was quite unhealthy before he discovered jogging so some say that it actually prolonged his life.

Garry Hoy

In 1993 the 38-year-old Toronto lawyer, described by a colleague as 'one of the best and the brightest', plummeted to his untimely demise from the twenty-fourth floor of the Toronto-Dominion Centre. He had thrown himself against a window in order to prove that the glass was unbreakable to a group of law students, who probably wondered if being a lawyer was all it was cracked up to be.

> **Common dangers in the home**
>
> 1. Slipping in the bath and banging your head
>
> 2. Falling over the dog
>
> 3. Not saying the right thing about your other half's new dress/hair implants
>
> 4. Missing any sort of special occasion because of a sporting event it clashed with
>
> 5. Assembling anything from IKEA and getting so irate you commit hara-kiri with a blunt screwdriver rather than face the full horror of assembling a wardrobe using their instructions

Fire or food?

There are already 6.6 billion of us in the world, which means not just good news for the sock industry but a happy business graph for undertakers. But which method of dealing with your remains is best for you?

Cremation

Ancient civilizations across Europe used to burn their dead, but Christianity banned it as it stuffed up their ideas on resurrection. Sir Henry Thompson, the queen's surgeon, was not happy with the shoddy state of packed British cemeteries in the nineteenth century and formed the Cremation Society in 1874, which has to be one of the most appealing names for a group and must have been turning eager applicants away in their droves. It was a full ten years before cremation became legal and the first crematorium was in Woking in England, where they know how to have fun.

Burial

Early evidence of burying the dead was found in European caves that dated from the Paleolithic period, when hirsute men weren't in touch with their feminine sides and deer looked nervous. People were buried on their own or with others and the communal burial pits were not always closed up. This was possibly so their slaves could be killed and join them, shouting 'the ungrateful bastard' as they went. It was those clever Egyptians who first thought of using coffins, which the Greeks and Romans took up with enthusiasm. But be that as it may, everywhere around the world, we're running out of room. Your burial will also inflict the duty of tending the grave on loved ones, who will have to fight the weather, vandals and really expensive flower shops to keep your final resting place looking scenic. And large family plots require careful thought too. Do you really want to spend eternity on top of your mother-in-law?

Top funeral songs

Forget Robbie William's 'Angels' and Elton John's 'Candle in the Wind' – you want your final audience to feel something other than the need to shower the pew in front with their breakfast. Choose from the following completely unsuitable options to make your final statement.

Very long

It's your last chance to bore the pants off everyone. If you didn't really like your young grandchildren anyway, these numbers will make them fidget until they explode.

1. 'Coma' by Guns N' Roses, at ten minutes and 13 seconds long, is guaranteed to put your nearest and dearest into one.

2. Jethro Tull's 1972 album, *Thick as a Brick,* is actually one song stretched over an entire album, lasting 43 minutes and 28 seconds – a good reason why the best flutes are those full of champagne.

3. 'The Devil Glitch' by Chris Butler is widely acknowledged as being the longest pop song ever at a whopping 69 minutes spread over 500 verses.

4. *Victory at Sea*, assembled by Richard Rogers and Robert Russell Bennett, was a 13-hour symphony composed for a historical documentary series on naval warfare (also called *Victory at Sea* and shown in the US).

5. Hook the church or crematorium up to the Internet for a thousand years of Tibetan singing bowls. 'Longplayer', essentially one song endlessly mixed up by a computer, started to play on 1 January 2000 and, barring severe global warming or someone getting really irritated with it, will continue to play non-stop until 31 December 2999, when it will come back to the point at which it began. Then it will begin again. It's also being played in Alexandria in Egypt and Brisbane in Australia, in case you fancy having your funeral somewhere a bit different.

Very wrong

1. 'Highway to Hell' by AC/DC will not only give the vicar a fright, but the audience will be put in mind of a man in a schoolboy's shorts and cap playing powerful guitar riffs. It could possibly work if you're a lifelong criminal or generally bad person.

2. 'Another One Bites the Dust' by Queen manages to neatly reduce the deceased to a statistic before you can say 'eight-hundred-degree oven'.

3. 'My Heart Will Go On' by Céline Dion is wrong on so many levels that it is almost right again. It will remind the congregation not only of the 1,513 souls who died on the *Titanic*, but also of the tragedy that their descendants had to listen to this absolute nonsense 85 years later. Freezing cold Atlantic, where is thy sting?

4. 'Stayin' Alive' by the Bee Gees – you couldn't and that's why all the teary faces are lining the pews and the worms in the cemetery are going haywire.

5. 'Don't Worry, Be Happy' by Bobby McFerrin would actually work a treat and put everyone in a sunny mood, heightened by serving rum at the wake. Well, who wants to live forever?

True stories about people's wills

- The famous author of *Treasure Island,* Robert Louis Stevenson, had a good friend named Annie Ide, who once had a bit of a moan that since she was born on Christmas Day she never had a really decent birthday party. So in a moment of genius he left his birthday on 13 November to Annie. He wrote in his will that since he no longer had any use for it, she should have it instead.

- Sandra West, a 37-year-old Beverly Hills oil heiress, left most of her $3 million estate to her brother-in-law, Sol, on the proviso that he ensured she was buried in her lace nightgown (normal so far) and her powder blue Ferrari (what!?) with the seat down. If he didn't do it, he would only get $10,000. Funnily enough, he complied. In a cemetery in San Antonio, Texas, concrete was poured around the Ferrari so nobody could dig it up and take her joyriding around Beverly Hills in her nightie.

- An amiable Australian named Francis R. Lord left one shilling to his beloved wife in the hope that she would catch a tram 'so she can go somewhere and drown herself'. She never claimed it.

- In Cherokee County in North Carolina a woman left her entire estate to God. This caused a headache for the county sheriff, who was ordered by the court to try and find the beneficiary. A few days later, the possibly weary sheriff returned and gave them the lowdown in a report: 'After a due and diligent search, God cannot be found in Cherokee county.'

- Florence Nightingale, who was revered for soothing brows in the Crimea and wandering around with a lamp without setting fire to anything, wanted to leave her body to science. Science didn't get to hear about her request and she was buried with her parents in St Margaret's Church in East Wellow, Hampshire. The church still commemorates her birthday on the second Sunday in May with a service and a good buffet.

And finally...

Hell

For a start, hell is actually meant to be a bit of a laugh. Sure, the eternal damnation gets a bit trying around the 400-year mark, but look at the positives; you'll never need a blanket round your knees again, you get to poke Pol Pot with a hot poker and elaborate celebrations are already being planned for when George W. Bush and Tony Blair check in.

Heaven

If you reach the Pearly Gates and there is a note saying 'Back in five minutes', do not be alarmed. Wait patiently and don't touch anything.

Chapter Seventeen

Keep Alive

(Or Keep Fit If You Are An Optimist)

There are a number of different ways to escape the fatty folds of your favourite chair and keep fit as you get older. Yes, the chair is your friend and is there to support you but if you spend too long in it and not enough outside doing something active, it will come back to bite you on your (now ample) behind.

Exercises for the partially knackered

At home

If you are living on a shoestring, you might not want to go to the expense of joining a gym. You might also not want people to watch you flying backwards off the running machine after you press the wrong button. Here are some tips for exercising around the home:

Nodding your head in time to music

Good for relieving tension in the neck as well as getting a dose of culture and infusing a sense of learning in the house. You may also want to swing or tap a shoe, but don't get carried away.

Washing the dog

This may seem like a trivial exercise but you would be surprised how many calories you will burn giving the pooch a good shampoo, especially if you use conditioner as well. The effort is greatly increased if you have to chase the little so-and-so round the garden for an hour beforehand.

Watching football

It's a dangerous business being an armchair football fan, and it does not get better with age. England player Rio Ferdinand once injured himself reaching for the remote control and he's just a youngster. Fans most frequently suffer from neck, back and shoulder sprains when they leap from their chairs to celebrate a goal. It actually puts people in hospital every year. Here are four stretches that will help keep you as lithe as an eel:

The elbow flare – this has nothing to do with those bad trousers from 1964 that you still wear. It's also called the 'executive stretch', which sounds like something from a Hong Kong massage parlour. Put your hands behind your neck and lightly clasp your hands together, with both elbows pointing forwards. Then squeeze the muscles between your shoulder blades and flare both elbows out either side of you – be careful not to knock books off a nearby shelf or hit your spouse in the face if they are standing beside you.

Chest stretch – standing up with knees slightly bent and toes pointing forward, reach back, clasp your hands together and feel your chest area stretch as you calmly breathe in and out for around eight seconds. If you are a man, getting your wife to do this so you can ogle her accentuated bosom is considered part of the fun. If you are a woman and your man is a bit chubby, ditto.

Lumbar stretch – lying on your back, put both hands on your legs just below your knees, then gently pull both knees toward your chest, keeping your lower back in contact with the floor. Hold for half a minute. Relax, get up, wander round, have a quick look at the post, realise it is all junk mail mainly selling beige underwear. Now repeat. Do not confuse the lumbar with the rumba or you will end up in traction, spitting grape pips at your neighbouring patients for weeks.

The bean flick – to prevent injury when you are repeatedly opening cans of lager during important football games, warm up by getting a pile of dried beans, putting them on a chopping board and flicking them at high velocity, with whichever index finger you use to open cans of lager, into the garden or street below. Fully biodegradable, they will also feed the birds and you will develop a very strong finger that will remain injury-free throughout the World Cup or European Championships.

In the gym

Get out, give yourself an airing and engage with humanity. Just don't wander the changing rooms in the nude and put the regulars in therapy.

Yoga

Great for balancing mind and body and doing a spot of self-realisation on a Tuesday evening, this ancient Indian system of philosophy has been traced back to around 1500 BC. In the West, it is most commonly associated with tricky postures and deep breathing. Hatha yoga is the best-known and Ashtanga yoga works by sweating as a form of detoxification. Go easy on the garlic the night before.

Pilates

In the 1920s, German gymnast Joseph Pilates came up with an exercise-based system, originally called Contrology, which aimed to develop the body's core. He had been rather poorly as a child and wanted to improve his own strength and fitness. This he did in style, going on to be handy at boxing, diving and martial arts. Pilates creates a stable bodily centre for various kinds of movement, toning and stretching the muscles so that your skeleton gets back into balance and you feel rather fine afterwards. It's also great for back problems and arthritis. Buy yourself a roll mat and give it a whirl. You may notice a lot of people in their sixties tend to cheat by doing the exercises as quickly as possible instead of slowly, which works the muscles far more. Do not report them to the teacher – you will be labelled a sneak and duffed up in the car park.

The great outdoors

Walking

Nobody is certain why, but old-timers love to walk. Maybe it is because it is gentle on the joints and possibly because it is free. But stick a pin in any fell or woodland on a map and nearby will be octogenarians stamping the turf and chattering about their latest hiking trip to New Zealand's South Island. There is a ritual to the way these enthusiasts pack a simple, earnest lunch of sandwiches and cake, load a thermos with tea before waterproofing the dog and embarking on a 15-mile assault on some distant and mist-shrouded peak. See www.ramblers.org.uk for inspiration.

Self-defence

If you are going to be out and wandering the neighbourhood, you might run into the scourge of the modern age: the hoodie. As clothing, hoodies are an ironic garment of the twenty-first century.

Loosely classed as sportswear, the nearest the scowling criminal minority who wear them come to sport is when they steal people's bicycles and get chased by the police. Experts say the best form of self-defence is to run when gangs of hoodies are closing in, but with your dodgy knees and general lack of stamina you might not even make it to the laundromat on the corner. Instead, have a few moves up your sleeve along with those used tissues.

The 'hoodie' wink

A classic move, all you have to do is distract the hooded assailant for a moment, possibly with a line like 'that old woman over there has just collected her pension'. When he or she looks away, yank the hood down over their head and run for it in the other direction.

The Samson

Just as the great warrior was undone by losing his locks, so the hoodie has an Achilles' heel. As the would-be attacker moves in, if his or her hooded top is unzipped, dance nimbly to the left using the agility you have learned while waltzing, circle round behind them and in one slick move pull their hooded top off from the back. Their powers will quickly fade and they will slink off in defeat.

Go mobile

Get in close and seize their mobile phone. With their communications shut down, they can't call reinforcements on undersized bicycles and will soon miss listening to their idiotic ringtones so much that they will fall to the ground, weakened to the point of surrender.

Give them stick

If you carry a walking stick or a cane, learn how to use it. Kevin Garwood of Great Yarmouth in England did exactly that. A black belt in judo and karate, he teaches the aged how to use a stick to defend themselves and it is very popular and effective. Using strangleholds, arm locks and throws, one of his pupils successfully stopped two yobs from trying to steal her handbag. Grey power!

The handbag

It's long been the source of an ASBO-wielding attacker's interest, and can be the weapon that defeats them. Swung with accuracy to the chin, it can prove a formidable foe. Reinforce the inside with chain mail and line it with small rocks for added weight and power.

The decoy bag

Instead of fighting them off, put up a valiant struggle for a few seconds and then release the bag, allowing the little darlings to escape down a side-alley and back to their dwelling to rummage through your possessions. This is when they trigger the hand grenade Uncle Bill left you in his will. The joy of tinkling glass and screaming in the distance is hard to beat.

The house keys

Your house keys could save your life one day. Getting your keys out of your pocket or handbag, carefully place a key between each knuckle of your clenched fist. If you don't have enough keys, one good, long jagged one gripped firmly and protruding from the side of your clenched fist will do. Now run like the wind and open your front door with them.

Chapter Eighteen

Old Spice

Is that a bottle of blood pressure pills in your pocket or are you just pleased to see me? It's a touchy subject with people in their silver years, but no handbook would be complete without mentioning this important part of our lives, the reason we all came to be here in the first place – sex. Recent research has found that older people who have sex regularly enjoy a superior experience and are mentally and physically better off. There is also evidence that points to people who have more sex living longer. So come and put some kink in your wrinkles.

Zimmer frame Kama Sutra

Loosely translated from Sanskrit, *Kama Sutra* means 'book of love'. It is an ancient Hindu text on how to do it in colourful and different ways, which has kept schoolboys sniggering in bookshops for decades. Here are six positions for you to try:

The begonia

Like the lotus position but different. The man sits with his ankles crossed on the floor (put a mat down) and the woman sits on top of him, wrapping her legs around his back. Talking about what plants you should put in the herbaceous borders next spring will get you both in the mood in no time. The Zimmer frame should be left to one side but close to hand in case of severe stiffness. You don't want to have to call for help.

The twinings

Similar to the twining position, this works well for beginners who are just getting to grips with the *Kama Sutra*. The theory is that you lie on your sides, get entangled and take it from there, basically having a bit of how's-your-father sideways. Keep the Zimmer frame close by and use it to haul yourself up again. Then go and have a lovely pot of Assam.

Driving the pig home

Like the position called driving the peg home, but for when the man in the partnership has behaved disgracefully, preferably at a public function like a christening party, and is being driven home by an angry wife who is telling him there will be no hanky-panky for a very long time. The Zimmer frame is shut in the boot but can hear every word.

First posture of the perfumed window box

This is similar to the first posture of the perfumed garden but for those with space restrictions. The man is on top in the missionary position with the woman's legs raised either side of him. And the window is open. Note: even if you have a garden, no self-respecting old-timer should be out there practising the *Kama Sutra* if your neighbours can see you. They will be scarred for life. Instead, take the Zimmer frame for a brisk canter around the garden if you are still feeling frisky.

The posture of the imbalance

Like the posture of the balance, when the man sits on the edge of the bed and the woman, facing away, lowers herself onto him and balances on his penis, using his knees for support. Use the Zimmer frame in front of her for additional support.

The position of the seaside resort

You don't really want to go to South America as much these days what with the carbon footprint and the time difference, which is why this position is close to the position of the Amazon but with less flying involved. The man sits in a chair and the woman sits side-saddle across him. The Zimmer frame is not required but is always comforting to have nearby. Of course, you can still have fun with a bit of personal Brazilian deforestation.

Late dating

You are never too old to get out there and cause a bit of intrigue and scandal while getting the children worried about rash alterations you might make to your will. But there are numerous pitfalls to avoid.

Men

Do say: 'You have great teeth.'
Don't say: 'Where did you buy them?'

Do say: 'That's a lovely dress.'
Don't say: 'You look hot in surgical stockings.'

Do say: 'Would you like to join me for lunch next Thursday?'
Don't say: 'Can you wear those beige tights that hold the bulges in?'

Women

Do say: 'And this must be your son?' (On bumping into an old boyfriend out walking with a teenager who looks a bit like him.)
Don't say: 'And this must be your grandson.'

Do say: 'It's nice to have a man about the house.'
Don't say: 'What do you mean you can't install the Digibox?'

Do say: 'It's very common.'
Don't say: 'I have some horse-strength Viagra at my place.'

Really bad ideas for dating:

- Anything that involves taking your grandchildren to some form of amusement

- Anything involving spaghetti

- Zorbing

- Bungee jumping on the same cord

- Theatres where they invite members of the audience to join the actors onstage

- A scenic helicopter ride on a windy day after a large hamburger

- Films with lurid sex scenes

- Just after a vasectomy

It's all about the location

Here are some top places to strike up a conversation with someone in the hope of finding a deep, meaningful relationship full of happy memories and shared experiences. Or just someone to have fumbles with during *EastEnders*.

The bus

When waiting for the bus, quickly scan the others for potential targets. Is he quite old? He'll sit at the front, then. Is she in her sixties? She's almost certainly a middle-of-the-bus kind of girl. Do not lurk at the back and try and make a pass at teenagers – you will get arrested.

The supermarket

Hang around in the frozen food section, and when a lovely-looking candidate comes into view, wave a TV dinner in front of them, look a bit confused and ask them if they know how long you cook beef stroganoff for one. They will take pity on you and invite you round for a spin with their microwave. Works every time.

The Internet

One of the world's largest online dating websites, www.match. com, claims that most of its users are over 50. Spurred on by the thought of never having to leave their own home and being able to meet people while in their pyjamas (or worse), a flotilla of silver surfers have set sail on the sea of electronic mating. Just don't catch a nasty virus.

Keeping things spicy

- Roleplay – imagine you are young, virile and able to stay awake for more than ten minutes

- Throw a vicars and tarts party – invite real vicars to mix it up a bit

- Invite friends round to play strip Scrabble – just don't tell them until you have locked all the doors and cut the phone line

Chapter Nineteen

Fruit of Your Loins

Where would you be without your children? Apart from richer, happier and more relaxed? Yes, they are extraordinarily difficult as babies, but gradually they start to sleep at sensible times, become continent, begin earning their own money and eventually flee the nest, leaving some parents strangely bereft and others quietly popping champagne corks. As you head into your golden years, your children and grandchildren will present a whole new range of joys and disasters. But one day, when you have gone mildly loopy, they will be back in charge.

How to put the children off coming to stay

If you have a big enough house and they live quite far away, usually they will want to come and stay the night. Maybe two if you have bathed recently. Sometimes this will be welcome, sometimes not. If you were looking forward to watching videos of *Miss Marple* all weekend, put them off with an unsuitable excuse:

1. The dog has eaten something foul and is defecating uncontrollably. The smell is so bad the vet nearly passed out.

2. There has been an outbreak of avian flu at the nearby swan sanctuary and the police have set up a 5-mile exclusion zone. You had swans in the garden only last week and you had remarked on how they seemed to be behaving oddly.

3. The house has been destroyed in a very localised tornado, which the media hasn't reported.

4. Your foreign exchange student they didn't know was lodging with you seems to be displaying symptoms of Ebola fever.

5. Don't answer the phone, and switch off your mobile. The only snag is they may get worried and call the emergency services. If an ambulance turns up, play dead and hope you don't wake up in a small, dark fridge without your kidneys.

How to get them to emigrate really far away

1. 'How extraordinary! In Manly in Sydney, you can live by the beach but be at the Opera House in twenty minutes on the fast ferry. Imagine that.'

2. 'Someone at the pub the other day told me that nannies are really affordable in Nicaragua.'

3. 'The Cook Islands are meant to be nice, with lots of good seafood and diving. It's a long way but we will come and visit.'

4. 'Vancouver has got loads of outdoors activities, from skiing to kayaking. The kids would love it.'

5. 'It may be the most dangerous country on the planet, but you can do worse for affordable housing than look to Afghanistan.'

How to cope with...

Christmas

This is the big one. Forget commemorating the birth of Jesus. Christmas is the time when that argument you had over whose fault it was the turkey got burned in 1974 resurfaces. Bad vibes fuelled by alcohol can reach epic proportions, with the added danger that the day is centred around the kitchen, which is full of sharp knives and highly volatile people trying to ignite equally flammable brandy. Get out of the cooking by entertaining any offspring and get out of everything else by feigning a funny turn. Or just duck out of the whole ghastly affair and go and feed soup to the homeless. At least they say 'thank you'.

Try this: fake a heart attack and then get the ambulance to drop you off at home. Open your rather expensive bottle of Puligny-Montrachet that you were saving for a special occasion and settle down in front of *The Eagle Has Landed*.

Easter

It might well be the most important annual occasion for Christians when they commemorate the Resurrection of Christ, but it is also a dangerous mix of a few days off and unlimited chocolate. Consequently, families can rub against each other like angry clouds until the thunder starts to rumble.

Grandchildren will be absolutely wired on the chocolate and will need pacifying with walks in the countryside, which is a safe way of breaking up the group dynamic.

> **Try this:** take a painting holiday in the south of France instead. Nobody will try and join you.

Family holidays

Short-haul is favourable when your grandchildren are small. Beach holidays are excellent with their simple recipe of sun, sea and sand. They also have a knack for providing enough booze for everyone to be utterly anaesthetised throughout the whole dreadful thing, and often have crèches and clubs for children. Long-haul needs careful thought as it has the additional trauma of everyone feeling like they have just landed on the moon and haven't slept since last week. Power-napping on the flight is essential to combat a potential fracas upon arrival. 'Accidentally' book yourself into a hotel with a similar name that is several miles in the opposite direction and spend the rest of the holiday actually enjoying yourself.

> **Try this:** plead poverty and duck out of it. If your children really want you to come they will pay for you, meaning you will be in a good mood for the whole time as nothing can puncture the joy of a free holiday.

Grandchildren proofing

You have worked long and hard to get the house looking its best, with precious family heirlooms on the mantelpiece and your finest china in the glass-fronted cupboards. Then your marauding grandchildren appear, making the Visigoths look like a particularly placid version of *Swan Lake*, hell-bent on getting their sticky paws on everything valuable and smashing most of it in the rush. Keep your vases intact by:

1. Putting them in the garden – the children, not the vases. If it is the middle of winter and freezing cold, justify this by telling their parents it will make them stronger. Point to their red faces when you allow them back in five minutes before they are driven away and say, 'There! Now they have got some colour in their cheeks.' Be warned: they will hate you for this.

2. Putting them to work. If you are cooking, get the grandchildren to help with any vegetable preparation beforehand, teach them silver service as 'it might come in handy when you are a student' and get them to work as waiters and waitresses at the table. Provide uniforms and make sure they're not sitting outside the back door, having a moody cigarette and bitching about the pay.

3. Teaching them to knit and mend. Then next time they come round sit them down with any socks that need repairing. If they still misbehave, make sure the socks are unwashed. They will not want to visit grandpa and grandma's any more.

4. Telling them if they misbehave they will have to cut your toenails. This could backfire if they actually want to do it. If this happens, give them clippers, not scissors, if you value your toes.

5. Clearing your house of anything of any value whatsoever. The grandchildren can't smash anything, burglars can't steal anything and you can claim you have gone minimalist to puzzled visitors.

Top answers for smart-arse grandchildren's questions

'Why is the sky blue?'
What you should say: 'It's to do with Rayleigh scattering, which was studied by Lord Rayleigh, a British physicist. Light consists of electromagnetic waves and the distance between two crests of a wave is called the wavelength. The amount of light that is scattered depends on the wavelength of that colour. The dust and vapour in the atmosphere selectively

scatters the light rays, and blue light is scattered more than other light frequencies.'

What you will say: 'Because it is.'

What you would like to say: (if during a car journey) 'I want total silence until we arrive.'

'What does Mummy mean when she says you are having a male menopause, Grandpa?'

What you should say: 'Well, the word "menopause", loosely translated from the Greek, means "cessation of month". And men don't get periods so that is not why I have bought a Dodge Viper and have a girlfriend who is thirty years younger than me.'

What you will say: 'Your Mum is being funny again.'

What you would like to say: 'Just you wait until you get to my age.'

'Why do I have to eat my greens?'

What you should say: 'Because fresh fruit and vegetables are an essential source of Vitamin C, which is vital for your development and health.'

What you will say: 'Because they will make you grow big and strong.'

What you would like to say: 'Because if you don't you could get scurvy, which is when you feel weak and your joints ache, you get liver spots on your skin, healed scars reopen and your gums bleed. More broccoli?'

'Why don't you live in a bigger house, Grandma?'
What you should say: 'It's not the size of your house that matters, but that you are healthy, happy and loved.'
What you will say: 'Because when our children moved out, we didn't need so many bedrooms.'
What you would like to say: 'We live in a smaller house than you but at least we own it. In the next recession you and your parents are going to end up in cardboard boxes under a bridge.'

'Why is your hair so grey?'
What you should say: 'Because my hair follicles produce less pigment as I get older.'
What you will say: 'Er, because I am getting older.'
What you would like to say: 'Because I am permanently worrying about whether you bunch of miscreants are going to end up being responsible adults.'

Youth of today – a glossary

Parents and grandparents have always struggled to understand what younger people are talking about, but with the rapid technological and cultural changes of the twenty-first century it's now harder than ever. Is it rapper slang or Creole patois? Who knows? Phrases they might come out with include:

Your mother – a retort if someone is being rude to you. It's faintly hinting at unsavoury suggestions about the other person's mother. This can be doubly useful for old-timers as your peers' mothers will often be dead too.

Wagwaan – what's going on? What's up? This is derived from Jamaican patois.

Vexed – irritated. One word you will know that has come full circle.

Rents – parents. No sign of grandrents, so start a trend. It also sounds like 'ground-rent', which could be useful.

Scampi – a very attractive man. No longer a cheap meal with chips down the pub.

Book – it means cool. It comes from predictive text on mobile phones, when the first word that comes up when you type 'cool' is actually 'book'. Not to be confused with a collection of pages bound together and possibly containing knowledge that might further personal development.

Sick – something interesting or cool. As in, 'Those threads are really sick,' meaning, 'I like your clothes and wish to know which catalogue they came from.' So if you are in poor health, at least you will be hip with the youngsters.

Butters – someone or something that is ugly. The 't's are soft. Ignore imagery of toast. 'Those ladies at the village fete were butters,' therefore means 'Those ladies at the village fete were really ugly.'

Jack – not a nice boy's name. It means to steal something, and comes from carjacking.

Chirps – nothing to do with budgerigars. It means to chat up a member of the opposite sex.

Talk to the elbow – I am not listening.

Chapter Twenty

Technology

It isn't just what your grandchildren are saying that can be confusing. Technology is changing too. We have seen hydrogen and electric cars being touted as the way of the future. Phones have gone from big grey plastic things on the hall table to mobile ones that are small enough to floss your teeth with and can take pictures, play music and run the bath, hopefully not all at once. Almost as hard as understanding what young people are saying or why your pension is almost worthless, technology has moved along quicker than you can say 'Uniform Resource Locator'.

The Internet

One of the biggest recent changes has been the Internet, or web. Silver surfers have embraced this with an enthusiasm just the right side of mania, even if most of them don't know their ISPs from their JPEGs. But the important thing is that the rewired-retired are out there, surfing, buying, flirting and picking up killer tips on how to successfully grow clematis cuttings.

YouTube

Geriatric1927 is his user name, Peter Oakley is his real name. An 81-year-old from Leicester in the UK, he has posted a series of clips to the video-sharing website. Called *Telling it All*, each one is an insight into his rich and varied life, from his experience as a radar mechanic during World War Two to how much he likes motorcycles, which is a lot. His soft and mellow narrative style has awarded him the monicker: 'the coolest old dude alive', and in 2006 he meteorically rose to become the most viewed user on the site. Check out the wallpaper in his premier clip, *First Try*.

Chatrooms

Chatrooms are an emerging market for the elderly to get together for a virtual chinwag. Sites like www.sagazone.co.uk, www.notdeadyet.co.uk and www.oldmoaners.co.uk have chatrooms where you can reminisce about the good old days and grumble about the new. Just make sure you are not being chatted up by teenagers looking for a 'sugar grandaddy' or a 'yummy grandmummy'. If someone starts asking you what underwear you are wearing, tell them the truth. They will rapidly leave you alone.

Netspeak

If you get chatting with someone more web-savvy, they may bombard you with strange words and acronyms. Avoid trouble by knowing what they are talking about.

A/S/L – age/sex/location
Don't put 'ancient', 'yes please' and 'on the bed'.

GNOC – get naked on cam
Don't. Unless you are charging them lots of money.

NIFOC – naked in front of computer
Your computer didn't sign up for this. Do not join them.

TDTM – talk dirty to me
This phrase does not mean they want to know about the time you came in with your walking boots on and stamped mud into the shag pile carpet.

Mobile phones

Even the idiot-proof ones can seem complicated to sexagenarians who are just mastering the dark art of toasting waffles. Get your children or grandchildren to give you a tutorial. Sending your first text to your grandchild is a proud moment in any old-timer's book. However, you might want to save your soon-to-be arthritic fingers by using the following acronyms.

Text abbreviations for old-timers

imho – in my humble opinion

imlo – in my learned opinion

iirc – if I remember correctly

irrac – I rarely remember anything correctly

cya – see you later

cyab – see you at bingo

crm8 – cremate

kmt – kiss my teeth

kmtgaptiag – kiss my teeth goodnight and put them in a glass

aysos – are you stupid or something?

ia75gmab – I am 75 give me a break

iwdyiyimasa – I will disinherit you if you interrupt my afternoon snooze again

PINs and needles

Get your pin number tattooed on the inside of your eyelid. That way you will not be the geriatric holding up the entire queue in a supermarket, or standing for hours by a cash machine on a dangerous inner-city street at night trying to remember it. If using 'chip and pin' in a shop, it might bring to mind those first fumbles as a virginal teenager, mainly because you don't really know what you are doing, nobody has given you formal training or instruction and you haven't got a clue where the right buttons are.

Online banking

Grannies and grandpas are getting pretty nifty with paying bills and doing a bit of banking online. Look for the padlock symbol at the top right of the website address on your Internet window. No padlock, no good. 'Phishing' is a term used for leading you to fake sites that look official, where you surrender your bank details. Not to be confused with fishing, which involves more tench.

Digital cameras

All those boxes of pictures in the loft will soon be a thing of the past. When you die, your children just have to press delete rather than spend weeks in the roof fighting with spiders. Buy a digital camera, stick in a memory card and away you go. With unlimited photography, some of the pictures might not be of your thumb.

iPods, mobile devices and palmtops

Seriously, you want to learn about these? You only just realised the DVD player doesn't reheat soup.

Chapter Twenty-one

The Guide to Being a Grumpy Codger

Most people expect old-timers to be grumpy, partly because of the breakneck pace of technology and how much life has changed. It's what a lot of old-timers excel at doing. Look at Victor Meldrew in *One Foot in the Grave* – he was a black belt in grumpy. Clever scientists believe they know what causes it. IMS, or Irritable Male Syndrome, is a bit like PMT for middle-aged men, and is when their testosterone levels drop during the month. But regardless of this, people would be surprised to see the geriatrics beaming joyfully and skipping down the street. Make sure you conform to stereotype with the following:

1. The frown

Don't you just hate those idiots who tell you it uses 43 muscles to frown and 17 to smile? Tell them your face needs the exercise.

2. The grimace

It might be because you are in pain, or it might be because you have wind. But make sure you grimace at least 20 times a day. If a friendly stranger approaches, saying 'It might never happen', tell them it just did.

3. The mutter

If someone is getting on your nerves, for example, a shop assistant, walk off while muttering to yourself in dark tones. You might be using strong words to curse the day they were born or you might just be saying 'rhubarb rhubarb' but it will make you feel a lot better. The offending person will also feel hurt that you are saying unsavoury things about them. However, if they say 'Come back here and say that', your plan has struck the rocks and you should feign hardness of hearing.

4. The head shake

Similar to muttering, you can register your general dissatisfaction with the world by shaking your head. It suggests an overall air of unhappiness that the world today is not what it should be. If you were in charge, things would be markedly different. The fact that if you were in charge everything would be a great deal slower and would need eight different pills just to get started in the morning is irrelevant.

5. The tut

A vital tool in your repertoire of disgruntled noises is the humble tut. Strengthen yours using exercises such as rolling your 'r's, licking condensation off windows and always carrying a small bottle of water as a dry mouth can ruin the effectiveness. As can getting a tongue piercing. The tut is not to be confused with a series of hip hop dance moves of the same name, which involves making funny shapes with your arms.

Bitching for beginners

Make sure you have got a bit of practice in before you try these ideal subjects in a real-life scenario.

The price of things

Everything is more expensive – don't ever forget that you used to get a haircut for five shillings. These days people are not even certain if shillings are a disease or if it is where they went skiing in Austria last year. You bought your house for £60 back in 1959 and, whatever happens, you will not move on. Moaning about cost can usefully be included under the banner 'Rip-off Britain', which can be doctored to encompass anything from the price of butter to the latest rise in tobacco prices.

Youth of today

Dreadful and responsible for most crime, this is the reason why National Service should be reintroduced. Hoodies are obviously the worst, followed by chavs and general low-lifes, swearing and drinking in public, boys fighting, girls wearing tarty outfits and teenage pregnancy. The list is virtually endless, and the good news for the avid moaner is it is getting worse because the government doesn't have a notion how to deal with it. Send them to a holiday camp for smashing up your car? Genius.

Global warming

The gradual plundering of the Amazon in the name of growing more soya beans is a ripe topic for discussion. By 2080 the temperature might have risen by between 2 and 4 °C, meaning very high seas and soggy pants. You get to have the last laugh, though, because although it's a fine subject to get maudlin about, you won't be around to witness everyone thrashing about like beached haddock when the air finally runs out.

Tax

It's risen. Politicians have gradually closed all loopholes and now people are living to work, not working to live. You slaved away for decades doing a job you hated and now you want to vent spleen and tell everyone about it. The plus side is everyone of a working age will agree with you and offer to drive you to London so you can poke the Chancellor in the eye with a sharpened umbrella.

Pensions

The UK has the lowest-value pensions in Europe so you are totally justified in getting fired up over this one. You worked hard for years and now you are having to barbeque the cat and burn the furniture just to stay alive. It's a sad fact that successive governments are all as bad as each other, and politicians are mainly a collection of power-crazed swine.

Chapter Twenty-two

Nostalgia

It sounds like a medical complaint but sometimes we can't help having an attack of nostalgia. At least it is more enjoyable than angina. There are times of reflection when it's hard to let go and move on in life, but you don't need to let go completely. Childhood games like cat's cradle will sort out your arthritis, and kick the can will put you straight back in touch with your inner child – and straight back in hospital if you run too fast.

Games

Blind man's buff

Also known as blind man's bluff, this ancient game where you blindfold someone and they have to find the others is thought to have been played in Greece, about the time when the Romans were sharpening their swords and casting a malevolent eye over whole swathes of Europe. In France it is known as Colin-maillard after a French nobleman who, blinded in battle, fought valiantly on and hacked up a lot of people with his sword. And this was despite shouts of 'Watch out, you clumsy tit!' by his own men. The Tudors were also known to be fond of a game or two when things were slow, and Henry VIII's courtiers were meant to be pretty good at it. There is nothing like the thought of being beheaded to make you raise your game. It would probably be known as 'visually impaired deception' in these times of political correctness. It is beneficial for the elderly because it gets the heart going but doesn't involve too much exertion.

Cat's cradle

Excellent for keeping your hands nimble and your mind adroit, this game just requires a piece of string so it's cheaper than building a tennis court. Almost the moment string was invented, some show-off was doing funny things with it. It's played by looping the string in a series of patterns over the fingers and sometimes even joining up with other people's hands. Its exact roots are shrouded in mystery but the game is known across the world and is believed to be one of the oldest in existence. In Russia they call it 'the game of string', which took weeks to think up. Tying yourselves together and being unable to telephone for help is all part of the thrill.

Kick the can

Apart from being a nickname for dying, kick the can is a popular game. The idea is that you paint a can, bottle or bedpan a bright colour, place it in the garden or street and then get your assembled and aged friends to hide while you look for them. They have to try and run up and kick the can before you can get back to it. If the neighbours find you lurking in the rhododendrons, they may well phone for help. Hiding under parked cars is not recommended as you may become wedged or the car may drive over you.

Yo-yo

Some of the simplest pleasures in life, like feeding the birds or verbally abusing the prime minister when they appear on television, are the best ones. And the yo-yo is up there with them. The story goes that the yo-yo came from the Chinese but was first mentioned in ancient Greece in 500 BC, where they were made from terracotta discs. Examples can still be found in the National Museum of Athens in Greece. But the yo-yo really came into its own in the 1920s. They were very popular in the Philippines, and in 1928 they started being produced in the US by an American-Filipino called Pedro Flores. After World War Two, the toy that always comes back had a renaissance. Astronauts have studied them in space and 6 June is National Yo-Yo Day, in case you need an excuse to open some wine. If your arms need a bit of exercise, practise your sleeping, looping and 'walking the dog'.

Hula hoop

Across the centuries, children have entertained themselves with hoops and there is a good chance you were one of them. In the fifties, the whole world went mad for the humble hula hoop. The name arose from the resemblance to the Hawaiian *hula* dance, which was observed by British sailors in the nineteenth century, who got quite excited by it. But rolling vines, bamboo or anything else into a hoop and rotating it along the ground or slinging it around your waist has gone on for thousands of years. The ancient Greeks used to do it to keep fit, and this is still true today – it's great for exercise and even better for looking silly. And if you think your three minutes is quite impressive, the longest claim for continuous hula-hooping is 90 hours by Roxann Rose in 1987. She must have walked funny for days.

Remember when...

- Beer was 'one and ten' (one shilling and ten pence) a pint in 1956.

- A haircut was five shillings. Men went for a 'short back and sides'. And everyone spoke to one another. And barbers sold condoms.

- Sweet shops were an Aladdin's cave of big old jars containing things like mint humbugs and rhubarb and custard chews. And the man selling them wore a waistcoat and a bow tie and wouldn't stand any nonsense.

- Songs had words you could understand and a rhythm that you liked.

- When it used to snow properly at Christmas, not in April, and the snow was so deep in the garden you would lose the cat in a snowdrift.

- When summers were hot and seemed to stretch on forever, and ice creams melted quickly.

Old words and sayings to bring back

- 'Damn your eyes, sir.'

- 'You are a cur and a blackguard.'

- 'I saw her in the gloaming.'

- 'The council is threatening to oust us from our home.'

- 'Hearken, dearest. I hear the grandchildren approaching.'

- 'This iPod is a wizard invention.'

It's in the jeans

While getting nostalgic about your own past, at some point you will start to be interested in your family ancestry. As many old-timers get into genealogy, they soon learn that the family tree is not where you bury them when you can't take it any longer, it's a chart showing where you came from. In your thirties you really didn't give a monkey's why Uncle Cedric ended up moving to Arizona to start a chicken farm, but in your sixties the family history becomes increasingly significant. The easiest way to get started is online or through your local library.

Five things you might not want to discover about your family

1. It turns out that your great-grandmother wasn't an upstanding member of the community. She was suspected of beating a man silly in a pub brawl, although she was never convicted, and in one old newspaper article you discover she is described as 'a septic malingerer whose gin-breath is nearly as vile as her language'.

2. Your Great Uncle Wilfred didn't decide to start a new life in Australia at all. He was shipped there for nicking stuff.

3. Your great-grandfather was once found in bed with a llama in Argentina. He claimed they were sharing body heat to keep warm.

4. Somebody's grandmother ran a bordello in Texas. On the upside, it was reputed to be the best one in town and they had a real bath.

5. You actually have a brother and a sister you didn't know you had, living in Kent and working in the food industry and education respectively. Your inheritance has just been neatly carved into three.

Chapter Twenty-three

Famous Last Words

As we shimmy disgracefully towards the closing of *The Deranged Book for Old-timers*, the overwhelming desire is to end with something poignant, the suitable full-stop rather than an inadvertent cry of 'Who stole my underpants?' And what more interesting way than perusing the final words of the famous? Just remember that what they actually said as they died was probably 'Urrrrrrrrrgggggghhhhhhhhhh' – but who needs reality when you can have humour?

'All right then, I'll say it: Dante makes me sick.' Lope de Vega, 1562–1635. One of the founders of Spanish drama, the Madrileño playwright and poet apparently revealed his true feelings about the Italian poet from Florence upon being told his end was near.

'Either that wallpaper goes, or I do.' Oscar Wilde, 1854–1900. Actually called Fingal O'Flahertie Wills, he lived out his days in exile in France and is buried in Père Lachaise cemetery in Paris.

'I am dying. Please… bring me a toothpick.' Alfred Jarry, 1873–1907. The French surrealist writer had a love for the strange.

'Don't let it end like this. Tell them I said something.' Francisco 'Pancho' Villa, 1878–1923. The Mexican revolutionary tried to take over the Mexican Revolution but ended up just causing trouble in New Mexico and Texas instead.

'It's very beautiful over there.' Thomas Edison, 1847–1931. An industrious sort, he held the patents for over 1,000 inventions and once said that genius is 'one per cent inspiration and ninety-nine per cent perspiration'. It's not known where he was referring to, but it might well have been the Seychelles.

'Bugger Bognor.' King George V, 1865–1936. Apparently, his doctor said he would soon be fit enough to go for a visit, but the king felt otherwise about the fashionable seaside resort.

'I should have drunk more champagne.' John Maynard Keynes, 1883–1946. The British economist was responsible for altering the way governments tackled unemployment.

'Go away. I am all right.' H. G. Wells, 1866–1946. Herbert George Wells, who liked to pen a bit of science fiction, has a statue of a *War of the Worlds* tripod in Woking in his honour. You get the feeling Woking is where it all happens.

'I should never have switched from Scotch to Martinis.' Humphrey Bogart, 1899–1957. The stellar actor's middle name was DeForest, and in World War One he served in the Navy, sustaining an injury which paralysed his upper lip.

'Is everybody happy? I want everybody to be happy. I know I am happy.' Ethel Barrymore, 1879–1959. Winston Churchill once proposed to the Academy award-winning actress but she turned him down.

'I've had a hell of a lot of fun and I've enjoyed every minute of it.' Errol Flynn, 1909–1959. The swashbuckling Australian was rather into the drug-taking, women and booze. No wonder he sounded chipper.

'Am I dying or is this my birthday?' Lady Nancy Astor, 1879–1964. During her last illness, she briefly woke to find the whole family clustered round the bed looking a bit worried. As the first female MP, she liked to have a joust with Winston Churchill. She once said to him: 'If you were my husband, I'd put arsenic in your coffee.' To which the big fellow famously replied: 'Madam, if I were your husband, I'd drink it.'

'Money can't buy life.' Bob Marley, 1945–1981. In 2001 the Rastafarian reggae icon was awarded a star on the pavement in Hollywood.

'It's all been rather lovely.' John Le Mesurier, 1912–1983. Thank goodness Sergeant Wilson from *Dad's Army* decided to stop working as a solicitor's articled clerk and trained as an actor.

'Love one another.' George Harrison, 1943–2001. Trust one of The Beatles to deliver such a sublime line. Reports that his family immediately started fighting over the inheritance are unfounded.

'I can't believe after all this time it was a bloody banana that killed me.' Ivanka Perko, 1933–2006. This Slovenian woman had fled with nothing but the clothes she was wearing to a better life in Australia. She dropped a banana on her leg and, suffering from a delicate skin condition, died from the scratch it caused. Apparently she was being funny to the end.

Author's Last Word

(which is a remote prospect as he never shuts up)

Finally, after getting a bit reflective on life, we reach the end of the journey. Not of life, just this book – where a spot of *Last of the Summer Wine* and a good snooze are the just deserts of the weary reader. The path has been long, risky and has occasionally involved swearing, but somehow we have got there in one piece and smelling of blueberries. We have engaged, we have shared and we have seen how to make dangerous cocktails. But most importantly of all, we have learned why we don't keep elephants. May your days be sunny and your taste in pets sensible.

M. W.

The End